# An Introduction to Standards-Based Reflective Practice for Middle and High School Teaching

# An Introduction to Standards-Based Reflective Practice for Middle and High School Teaching

ELIZABETH SPALDING
JESUS GARCIA
JOSEPH A. BRAUN

Teachers College, Columbia University
New York and London

Published by Teachers College Press, 1234 Amsterdam Avenue, New York, NY
10027

*Library of Congress Cataloging-in-Publication Data*

Spalding, Elizabeth, 1951–
    An introduction to standards-based reflective practice for middle and high
  school teaching / Elizabeth Spalding, Jesus Garcia, Joseph A. Braun.
      p. cm.
  Includes bibliographical references and index.
  ISBN 978-0-8077-5055-1 (pbk. : alk. paper)
    1. Middle school teachers–Training of. 2. High school teachers–Training of.
  3. Middle school education–Philosophy. 4. Middle school education–Standards.
  5. High school education–Philosophy. 6. High school education–Standards.
  I. Garcia, Jesus, 1941–  II. Braun, Joseph A., 1947–  III. Title.
  LB1776.5.S63   2010
  373.139–dc22                                                    2009046334

ISBN 978-0-8077-5055-1 (paper)

# Contents

## PART II: CLASSROOM CONTEXTS OF TEACHING

# Dedication to
# Richard R. Powell

Richard Powell was to have been the third author of this book. He passed away in 2003. Richard's death was a shock to the many people who knew and cared for him as a friend and colleague. Richard, Jesus, and Liz met at Indiana University in Bloomington, Indiana, where Jesus was on the faculty in the College of Education and Richard and Liz were doctoral students in the Department of Curriculum and Instruction. Richard was completing his studies as Liz was beginning hers. She followed his footsteps into a challenging graduate assistantship. She admired his keen intellect, his extraordinary work ethic, and his quirky sense of humor. During Richard's years at Indiana and beyond, Jesus was his friend and mentor. The three of us shared a commitment to teacher education and to multicultural education.

The idea for a book developed over time during casual and professional conversations: Jesus, Richard, and Liz wanted to write a general methods book that personalized and contextualized the content and that encouraged preservice teachers to grow by reflecting on their own autobiographies. Work on the book kept us connected for several years as we migrated to various universities to pursue our professional goals. Liz continued to view Richard as a role model, for he compiled an impressive record of academic accomplishments in just a few short years. We fully expected that Richard would contribute his scholarship, insight, and passion for the cause of equity to this book. Tragically, he did not live to fulfill the promise of his early career or to see the publication of *An Introduction to Standards-Based Reflective Practice for Middle and High School Teaching*. We miss him still.

# Acknowledgments

We would like to thank the many individuals who contributed to the successful completion of this project. We had the able assistance of University of Nevada, Las Vegas graduate students Irina Ionescu, Tiffany Hendrix, Lisa Coggins, Camille Calilung, and Yousef Bamahra. Frances Whited provided invaluable technical support. Novice and experienced teachers from across the country contributed their expertise and stories to this book. They include: Traci Mahone, Rae Burgess, Laura Barnum, Barbara Hull, Sandy Eichorst, Brian Kahn, Alena Dryden, Katie Bridges, and Linda Fussell. We are especially grateful to the middle and high school teachers in the Clark County School District who contributed reflective vignettes.

We are grateful to our families and friends who have listened to us patiently for several years and to our students and colleagues who have given us valuable feedback on drafts. Joseph Braun would like to particularly acknowledge the following: his wife, Anne Gosch, for her encouragement to complete this final book and the many years (and those to come) of love and being best friends; his sisters, Patricia Angely and Elizabeth Braun; Jeff Gray and Monty Dillard, his bandmates, who are like brothers; and, of special note, his daughter, Sage Elizabeth Gosch-Braun, and her recent decision after graduation from college to follow in his footsteps and become a teacher.

We thank the professionals at Teachers College Press, especially Marie Ellen Larcada, Karl Nyberg, Judy Berman, and Adee Braun.

# Introduction

*Always design a thing by considering it in its next larger context—a chair in a room, a room in a house, a house in an environment, an environment in a city plan.*

*—Eliel Saarinen, 20th-century architect*

It may seem odd to begin a book about education with a quotation by an architect. Yet, Saarinen's advice is as relevant to educators as it is to designers. A teacher's every action and belief is embedded and enacted in some context that begins in her personal identity and experiences and expands to include all the factors that influence classroom practice, from the students before her to the decisions of Congress.

*An Introduction to Standards-Based Reflective Practice for Middle and High School Teaching* is a contextualized guide to learning to teach in contemporary middle and high schools. Teaching is too often represented in texts as a decontextualized act. Over our years as teacher educators, we have grown increasingly uncomfortable with texts that describe teaching in abstract terms and in an impersonal voice. We have come to believe that a credible depiction of teaching must include descriptions of the professional daily work of teachers. Lists of general principles of teaching followed by recipes on how to implement particular teaching practices are less and less useful in today's diverse middle and high school classrooms, where the answer to so many questions is, "It depends." For that reason, readers will not find many "tear-out," "ready-to-use" worksheets or activities in this book. Our goal is to help teachers become reflective practitioners who decide which instructional materials and methods are appropriate with particular students, at a particular time, in a particular setting, for a particular purpose.

*An Introduction to Standards-Based Reflective Practice for Middle and High School Teaching* is a text for middle and secondary preservice teachers who are enrolled in a general methods course or other teacher preparation courses. This is an appropriate text for the majority of preservice teachers, who are still educated in traditional, full-time undergraduate programs. At the same time, we wrote this book with a broader audience in mind: individuals who enter teaching through 5th-year programs, graduate licensure programs, alternative route programs such as Teach for America, and district-sponsored programs designed to fill shortages in high-need areas. We recognize that such programs often compact the teacher education curriculum. For this reason, *An Introduction to Standards-Based Reflective Practice for Middle and High School Teaching* includes chapters on such topics as adolescent characteristics, classroom management, and working with the community. These topics may be the focus of separate courses in traditional programs but may be omitted from nontraditional programs if not covered in a single text. This book will help students in traditional programs to synthesize the various components of their teacher education curriculum. For students in nontraditional programs, this is a multipurpose text that focuses on methods of instruction. Finally, *An Introduction to Standards-Based Reflective Practice for Middle and High School Teaching* will be useful to novice teachers engaged in induction or mentoring programs and to any teacher interested in linking standards to reflective practice.

## CONCEPTUAL FRAMEWORK

In writing *An Introduction to Standards-Based Reflective Practice for Middle and High School Teaching*, we were guided by the following concepts:

- *Context*. In this book, we consider a teacher in a classroom, a classroom in a department, a department in a school, a school in a community, and so on. As Chapter 1 explains, one's teaching self exists in a variety of internal contexts as well (e.g., culture, gender, ethnicity, socioeconomic status). Students too must be considered in light of the contexts in which their identities are embedded.
- *Reflection*. John Dewey taught us that learning occurs through reflection. A half-century later, Donald Schön demonstrated that teaching is neither simply a technical skill that can be taught nor an innate gift that cannot be taught. Like architects, lawyers, doctors, and other professionals, teachers learn and refine their work through reflective practice. This book offers numerous examples of reflection by novice and experienced teachers and by the authors themselves.
- *Biography*. Self is one of the most important contexts of teaching, but one that is often overlooked in formal teacher education programs. Yet we know that the years spent in the apprenticeship of observation have a powerful influence on who we become as teachers. Reflection on our own sometimes limited educational

experiences is one way of growing beyond them. Even more likely to be omitted from formal teacher education is consideration of our own life experiences and how they influence our teaching selves. By providing examples of our own (the authors') educational and life experiences and how they have influenced who we are as teachers, we hope to model for readers the process of growth through reflection on biography.

- *Diversity*. This book is multicultural, but not in the traditional sense. We do not present a chapter on the disadvantaged or at-risk learner. Rather, we treat human diversity as an intellectual concept—not as a political imperative. The examples we use in the text—schools, classrooms, and students—convey to the reader that 1. diversity characterizes schools in the 21st century; 2. culturally relevant instruction is beneficial for all students; and 3. the educational community can better address the needs of minorities and other groups who traditionally have not performed well in schools.
- *Standards and Accountability*. The past decade has seen increased efforts at many different levels to implement standards and hold teachers and learners accountable to those standards. *An Introduction to Standards-Based Reflective Practice for Middle and High School Teaching* recognizes that reality by explicitly linking its content to the *Model Standards for Beginning Teacher Licensing, Assessment and Development* (1996). These standards were developed by the Interstate New Teacher Assessment and Support Consortium (INTASC) under the aegis of the Council of Chief State School Officers. In addition, the content of this book has been designed to help prospective teachers perform effectively in a standards-based teaching environment.
- *Authenticity*. This book is authentic on several levels. First, we have used our authentic voices throughout in an attempt to create a human relationship with our readers. Throughout the book, stories about and by teachers are authentic—not fabricated for the purpose of making a point in a textbook. We provide practical guidance, while remaining true to the authentic, complex nature of teaching. In other words, we hope we have fused theory with practice.

## ORGANIZATION OF THE TEXT

*An Introduction to Standards-Based Reflective Practice for Middle and High School Teaching* begins with the personal contexts of teaching. Chapter 1, "Becoming a Reflective Practitioner," introduces the concepts of reflection and biography, which influence the kind of practitioner one will become. Next, we focus on students–the context that matters most, to teachers (McLaughlin & Talbert, 1993). While some of the material in Chapter 2 might be considered review by students in more traditional programs, we believe that the questions of how we teach and what we teach cannot be separated from questions of who we are and whom we teach. Chapters 1 and 2 provide the context for the other topics and issues that follow.

Chapters 3 through 10 comprise the classroom contexts of teaching: managing the classroom, creating curriculum, planning for instruction, selecting instructional materials and strategies, teaching with technology, implementing instruction, and assessing learning.

The final two chapters focus on professional contexts of teaching: the community and the teaching profession itself. Chapter 11 asks the reader to consider the variety of communities that form a context for teaching. Chapter 12 ends the book as it began–with reflection on the nature of adolescence and on what it means to embark on a career in education.

## FEATURES OF THE TEXT

This text contains several features that we hope will personalize the content for the reader.

- *Reflecting on Practice*. Each chapter contains an autobiographical vignette by one of the authors, followed by questions that invite the reader to reflect on her/his experiences. Most chapters also contain at least one vignette by a practicing teacher.
- *Links to Model Standards*. We have included a number of ways to help preservice teachers begin thinking about the Model Standards (CCSSO, 1996) and thinking in ways that widely used teacher licensing tests require.

  *Marginal notes* call students' attention to content that is connected to the INTASC standards.

  *Standards-based matrix in the Appendix* references the content of the book to the *Model Standards*.

  *Up-to-date content* infuses the book. We have included timely topics such as *differentiated instruction, brain-based learning, strategies for working with English Language Learners, and the implications of No Child Left Behind for middle and secondary teachers.*

  *Two instructional methods chapters* divide methods (for purposes of discussion) into teacher-directed and student-centered.

# Part I

# PERSONAL
# CONTEXTS
# OF TEACHING

# CHAPTER 1

# Becoming
# a Reflective Practitioner

Teaching may appear to be a simple act conducted by a teacher equipped with a textbook in a classroom filled with students, but the reality is much more complex. Excellent teachers know themselves, their students, and their subject and how to teach it. But perhaps more important, they are reflective practitioners.

The overall purpose of this chapter is related to the following standard for beginning teachers: *The teacher is a reflective practitioner who continually evaluates the effects of his/her choices and actions on others (students, parents, and other professionals in the learning community) and who actively seeks out opportunities to grow professionally* (Standard #9, CCSSO, 1996). This standard is one of ten that describe what beginning teachers should know and be able to do upon completion of their teacher preparation programs. These standards were published by the Council of Chief State School Officers (1996) and are featured throughout this book to help you assess how you are progressing in your knowledge of teaching and learning.

Specifically, this chapter will help you:

- Embark upon the process of becoming a reflective practitioner through learning about yourself;
- Define reflection and explain how it can lead to more effective classroom practice;
- Use a variety of self-assessment and problem-solving strategies for reflecting on practice;
- Use information obtained from observation and research as a basis for experimenting with, reflecting on, and revising practice.

## HOW REFLECTION CAN IMPROVE TEACHING

Helping all students achieve high-quality learning outcomes should be the goal of every teacher. Reflection can help you meet this goal in several ways.

As you move through coursework and field experiences, you need to reflect on and question the ideas and beliefs that you bring with you to your teacher education program. For example, Ladson-Billings (2001) has shown that some teachers believe that working with poor children of color is "helping the less fortunate" (p. 82). Without reflection, teachers may not even be aware they hold such a belief, which impedes them from looking for the strengths in every learner. In addition, as a group of distinguished teacher educators recently stated: "The importance of learning about one's students is paralleled by the importance of learning about oneself" (Banks, Cochran-Smith, Moll, Richert, Zeichner, LePage, Darling-Hammond, & Duffy, 2005, p. 266). Through reflecting upon and questioning our life histories, experiences, identity, beliefs, attitudes, and dispositions, we can become aware of the differences and similarities between ourselves and the students we teach. Reflective teacher education can "help student teachers become more aware of themselves and their environments in a way that changes their perception of what is possible" (Zeichner & Liston, 1987, p. 25). Thus, reflective teacher actions lead to greater benefits for teachers and for all their students.

## CONSTRUCTING A TEACHING IDENTITY

Constructing a teaching identity is a fundamental part of learning to teach (Smagorinsky, Cook, Moore, Jackson, & Fry, 2004). That is one of the reasons that throughout this book we ask you to explore who you are, what you believe, why you believe it, and how that may influence who you will become as a teacher.

**CCSSO Principle 5: Motivation and Management**

Consider the following aspects of identity. You have your own distinctive personality traits, pet peeves, and idiosyncrasies. You are a product of a family in which you learned certain values and habits and from which you may have inherited physical characteristics or behavioral tendencies. Some parts of your identity derive from your religion, your ethnicity, your home language, your socioeconomic status, your gender, your educational experiences, the community, and the larger culture in which you grew up.

All these aspects influence how you will interact with students who bring equally complex identities into the classroom. Over the centuries, philosophers have stressed that knowing oneself is key to being fully human; likewise, educational scholars believe that knowing oneself is key to becoming an effective teacher (Bullough, Knowles, & Crow, 1991; Jersild 1955). Parker Palmer (1998), an educator and activist who has spent his career exploring the inner landscape of teaching, has urged teachers to inquire deeply into themselves:

Seldom, if ever, do we ask the "who" question—who is the self that teaches? How does the quality of my selfhood form—or deform—the way I relate to my students, my subject, my colleagues, my world? How can educational institutions sustain and deepen the selfhood from which good teaching comes? (p. 4)

Narrative and autobiography are powerful tools in helping individuals become reflective practitioners because they enable us to theorize about ourselves, learning, adolescents, and the role of schools in a democratic society, as well as pedagogy and classroom and school practices. These forms of story tap into pools of experiences that play significant roles in shaping our beliefs and attitudes toward teaching (Coles, 1989; Connelly & Clandinin, 1990).

Much research on teaching converges around the finding that teachers teach as they were taught. Before students even enter teacher education programs, most have spent at least 12 years in close company with teachers. From simple observation, prospective teachers have already learned classroom routines, styles of teaching content, ways of interacting with students, and other facets of what it means to teach. Lortie (1975) called this phenomenon the *apprenticeship of observation.*

The apprenticeship of observation is powerful, but it is susceptible to change. Prior educational and life experience are valuable resources for reflecting upon who one is as a teacher, who one wants to become, and why one may hold the beliefs that he or she does about teaching. Reflection upon experience is the first step in disrupting the apprenticeship of observation.

## REFLECTING ON LIFE EXPERIENCE

Throughout this book, we authors—Liz, Jesus, and Joseph—have included portions of our own teaching autobiographies. We share our vignettes to show you that we, too, are reflective practitioners. Our autobiographies model the process of reflection that we hope you will adopt as you read this book and throughout your career. We hope you will accept our invitation to compose your own teaching autobiography as you go through this book. As you read our introductory vignettes, consider how our school experiences influenced who we became as teachers.

### Liz Spalding: Analyzing a Role Model

Sister Judith was an English teacher in the small Catholic high school I attended. Although she had the reputation of being a "hard" teacher, about 25 of us courageous seniors enrolled in her elective World Literature class. Sister Judith insisted we take detailed notes on her scholarly lectures, although she didn't teach us how to do that. No one even dreamed of disrupting her lectures by talking or passing notes. Her essay exams were rigorous, as was her grading. Earning an "A" from Sister Judith was an accomplishment.

Eventually I became an English teacher myself. Although I had completed a teacher education program in which I was introduced to a variety of teaching strategies, I taught much as Sister Judith had. I lectured; I expected students to take notes; I gave essay exams. I often felt frustrated that many of my students were not learning and, worse, didn't seem to care. In my teacher education program I had learned many things: how to write objectives, plan a lesson, operate an overhead projector, create multiple-choice test items. But I had not learned the art of reflection–to question and evaluate the effects of my own decisions and actions in the classroom. Consequently, I was unable to identify the advantages and disadvantages of following in Sister Judith's footsteps.

Sister Judith knew her subject, cared about it passionately, and communicated that passion to us. She made her students believe we were capable of reading, understanding, and discussing sophisticated ideas and works of literature. She treated us as scholars and never lowered her expectations. This was the side of Sister Judith worth emulating.

What I did not realize then was that Sister Judith was primarily skilled at teaching students like me, who were already succeeding in school. She knew her students' names but not much more about us. Many students do not learn best from lectures, need to be taught note-taking skills, and may not read at grade level. Those students were not in Sister Judith's elite class–but they were in the classes I was teaching!

Had I been a reflective practitioner then, I might have been more selective about the qualities in Sister Judith I wanted to emulate. Instead, I replicated her methods of instruction without examining whether these methods were appropriate for the diverse students I taught.

## Jesus Garcia: One Teacher *Can* Make a Difference

I grew up and attended high school in the working-class community of Pittsburg, California. My parents had both immigrated from Mexico: my father was a steelworker and my mother was a homemaker. Not until I entered high school did I encounter a teacher who was Mexican American, like me. Mr. Leo Jimenez, a counselor at the high school I attended, was the only Mexican American on the faculty. Many of the minority students, Mexican and African American, gravitated toward him because he was "one of us" and, more important, because he showed an interest in us. Mr. Jimenez spoke Spanish with the Mexican American students and encouraged us to investigate our cultural heritage and to do well in high school so we could go on to college and serve as role models to other Mexican American students.

One day, Mr. Jimenez arranged a field trip for a group of students he had befriended. He drove us to see a tennis match between the Mexican American tennis great Richard "Pancho" Gonzalez and the equally great Lew Hoad. The highlight of the trip was having our picture taken with Mr. Gonzalez. Since I was one of the smaller students in the group, I stood next to the great athlete. What an experience! I learned first-hand that Mexican Americans were making significant contributions to the American experience, and I became convinced that I, too, could become someone like a Richard Gonzalez or perhaps a high school counselor.

Mr. Jimenez raised my consciousness in the areas of cultural diversity and community activism. While still in high school, I became concerned with the status of minorities. I wondered why minorities lived in one part of town, held many of the blue-collar jobs, and were only occasionally involved in political decisions affecting the greater community. I silently questioned why most minorities (myself included) were not in college preparatory classes, why there were few teachers of minority background, and why, as a senior, I was not encouraged to attend a college or university after graduation. I wondered out loud why Mr. Jimenez never became a principal or superintendent of a school district.

Eventually I became a classroom teacher. The students who walked into my classroom each year were unique individuals who brought their distinct personalities and a natural curiosity to the classroom. Regardless of their differences, they all desired attention and acceptance; they all wanted to be liked by other teachers, their peers, and me. All, in their own ways, asked me to prepare them to live in society.

Perhaps because I am of minority background and have been influenced by individuals like Mr. Jimenez, I was very conscious that my classroom behaviors could deny a student the opportunity to learn. And, like Mr. Jimenez, I took a special interest in helping minority students and others who had been marginalized in the education system. To this day, I detest the forces of discrimination that deny some students the opportunity to learn. A teacher's responsibility is to create learning environments where all students have the opportunity to learn and to grow intellectually.

## Joseph Braun:
## The Importance of Instructional Style for Individual Students

I saved all my report cards from first grade through high school and when I looked at them a few years ago I noted an intriguing pattern. When a teacher took particular interest in me as a person I tended to behave myself, and my academic potential was achieved—even with the strictest of fifth-grade teachers, Mrs. Hart. I remember her particularly because early in the school year she paid a visit to my home to tell my mother how well I was doing in her class. Her visit had a motivating effect on me and I did stellar work in school that year. But the year before and after fifth grade my grades took a nosedive. My relationships with my fourth- and sixth-grade teachers were challenging for me, my parents, *and* my teachers, because I acted out for attention, acceptance, affection, and approval. While well-intentioned, most of my teachers from fourth grade through high school resorted to fear and power as primary motivational tools to get their students to perform. I did not respond well in those situations. Occasionally, however, I encountered teachers like Mrs. Hart who used different approaches to help students learn, and as a result I would blossom.

Experience and reflection have helped me see that instructional style has implications for what students learn beyond the content you are teaching. Instructional style can affect how students feel about themselves as learners, you and the art of teaching, and your particular subject. Most of my teachers knew the content they were teaching. The difference was in how they approached helping students learn. The style of many of my college instructors was more humanistic: They took a genuine interest in each student and took time to know individual students personally. The teachers in my formative years relied on a more traditional style. They presented their content but retreated from more personal interactions with my classmates and me. My humanistic teachers worked to sell the subject matter to students by making connections between the content and applications to life. My traditional teachers presented their content without demonstrating how it could be personally meaningful. Finally, my humanistic teachers promoted success and continually sought ways to encourage slower students, as well as those learning more quickly, to do their best. My traditional teachers took a "sink or swim" approach.

***Questions to Consider.*** As you formulate answers for the questions below, consider what we authors learned from reflecting on our experiences with Sister Judith, Mr. Jimenez, and Mrs. Hart. These teachers affected us at different periods in our lives and for different reasons. All were quite different in their teaching styles. Notice that their influence on us extended far beyond the content they taught, shaping the ways we interact with students even today.

- How, if at all, were the three teachers described above similar? How were they different?
- Which of your former teachers made a difference in your life? What was the nature of this difference?
- Was the difference short-lived or lifelong?

- Did you turn to different teachers to meet different needs–academic, personal, social, and cultural?
- When you see yourself as a teacher, what do you see? Is that image based on a former teacher or teachers?
- What experiences in your life are motivating you to become a teacher?

## HOW REFLECTIVE THINKING
## SUPPORTS REFLECTIVE PRACTICE

John Dewey (1933) defined reflection as the "active, persistent, and careful consideration of any belief or supposed form of knowledge in the light of the grounds that support it and the further conclusions to which it tends" (p. 9). Reflective thinking begins with a state of uncertainty or confusion. The mind then searches for material that will resolve, clarify, or otherwise address the doubt. This material may consist of past experience or a fund of relevant knowledge. To be truly reflective, however, individuals must be willing "to sustain and protract that state of doubt which is the stimulus to thorough inquiry" (p. 16). While bringing quick closure to uncertainty may be more comfortable, it is not the best way to learn from experience. Teachers must also be knowledgeable about the traits and habits of individual students and of the entire environment that affects students in order to select educative experiences that nurture and sustain reflective thought.

### Theory into Practice: Reflecting on an "Unspecial" Student

Consider the journal entry below written by Ella Brown (a pseudonym), a preservice teacher during her placement in a rural/suburban high school. As you read, think about how Dewey's definition of reflection does and does not apply to this excerpt.

By observing the actions of his teacher and the principal, I noticed that Robert, even though he is a special student and needs special attention, received only negative attention. "Robert, be quiet," is a favorite saying for Mrs. X. . . . and it's always Robert who's being singled out, even when other students are being just as loud and unruly. . . . Now that I am leaving (this school), I am worried about Robert. . . . He took the news very hard. "I don't care anymore," he said. "You've helped me this far and now you're leaving. There's no way I'm going to pass. I can't do my work in class when everyone else is in there." And that's what makes me so angry. Robert

is in a class of 31 students. . . . [H]e has to push himself in order to
[pass] . . . but Robert will not push himself. He needs someone to
push him and support him and nurture him along the way. When
I'm gone, no one will push Robert. *No one.* (Spalding & Wilson,
2002)

***Questions to Consider.*** When she wrote this vignette, Ella had just finished
reading *The Shopping Mall High School: Winners and Losers in the Educational
Marketplace* (Powell, Farrar, & Cohen, 1986). According to these writers, the
"winners" in education are those who are designated as "special" for a variety
of reasons, such as disabilities, giftedness, or athletic prowess. The "losers"
are the "unspecial"–students who drift through high school like shoppers in
a mall, never "buying" or engaging in anything the school has to offer. Ella
made a connection between her reading and her experience observing in
classrooms.

- What was the source of Ella's uncertainty or confusion?
- What experience and knowledge did Ella draw upon in order to
  reflect upon Robert's situation?
- How did Ella resolve her discomfort? What more might Ella have
  done to further inquire into the case of Robert?

Just as Dewey has been fundamental to understanding the nature of reflective thought, Donald Schön (1987) has been fundamental to understanding
the nature of reflective practice. Schön argued that simply equipping teachers
with an array of instructional strategies was an inadequate approach to solving the complex problems of educational practice. He likened teaching in
some respects to an applied science, such as law, medicine, or management.
In other respects, he viewed teaching as an art, like painting, music, or dance.
All skilled professionals and artists possess the specialized knowledge of their
fields, e.g., a lawyer learns legal terminology and the procedures for arguing
a case before a jury. But lawyers also commonly face "unique, uncertain, and
conflicted situations of practice" (p. 22). When professionals meet problems
of practice, they reflect on, make explicit, and question their understanding
of their knowledge and actions in that situation. Schön called this "reflection-
*in*-action." Once the situation is past, the professional again examines his or
her knowledge and actions. This is "reflection-*on*-action."

In the case of Ella and Robert above, Ella wrote her journal while reflecting *on* action. That is, when she found a quiet moment outside the hustle of
the classroom, she used reflection to identify a pattern in Robert's behavior
and others' behavior toward Robert. She could potentially use that information to help Robert succeed academically.

### Theory into Practice: Reflecting on the First Year of Teaching

Kate Bell (a pseudonym) wrote the following journal entry during her first year of teaching. As you read, think about how Schön's definition of reflective practice does and does not apply to this excerpt.

> Reflection . . . Well, I use it all the time. After a lesson has flopped, I sit down and think about the organization, my expectations, my presentation of the task. . . . Usually, I can pinpoint where I went wrong and am able to make the lesson more successful with my next classes. . . . In addition, I use it in terms of classroom management. I remember how I dealt with distant and/or hostile students in the past and what worked and what didn't–I use it all the time. Every day. Without even being aware of it.

In this journal entry, Kate has managed to capture reflection-*in*-action ("I use it all the time . . . without even being aware of it") while reflecting *on* action ("After a lesson has flopped, I sit down and think about the organization, my expectations . . . "). Like the skilled professional Schön described, she uses the terminology of her field (e.g., classroom management, distant/hostile students) to describe her problem. Like the reflective practitioner Dewey described, Kate draws upon her fund of knowledge and experience ("what worked and what didn't") to solve problems.

Valli (1990) built upon Schön's work to create a hierarchy of reflection. The levels include:

- *Reflection in/on action* involves one's own teaching performance or observation of someone's teaching performance.
- *Deliberative reflection* involves "weighing competing claims or viewpoints."
- *Personalistic reflection* primarily concerns issues of personal growth and professional relations.
- *Critical reflection* requires considering the social and political implications of teaching and schooling, including the "possibility that schools are implicated in perpetuating an unjust social order" (pp. 219–221).

These levels of reflection are not discrete or exclusive. For example, in Ella's journal we see her reflecting on action, being deliberative as she describes the treatment accorded to Robert, and becoming critical of a school system that fails to provide the personalization Robert needs. Kate's reflection has personalistic elements as she describes her personal growth as a teacher and deliberative elements as she describes weighing in her mind the effectiveness of various strategies she has used in the past.

## Theory into Practice:
## Reflecting on the Political Implications of Schooling

Consider the journal entry below written by Maurice French (a pseudo-nym) during his placement in a high school social studies classroom.

> I am very patriotic and feel proud to stand for my flag . . . but I dis-agree with the principal's action [the high school principal entered the classroom and took down the names of students who did not stand during the Pledge of Allegiance]. Part of the reason we revere our flag is that it stands for freedom. What message does it send to young students learning about our liberties, when they are forced to stand for the flag? Does it not defeat the purpose of pledging alle-giance to our flag, if we are forced to do so against our will?

What levels of Valli's typology do you see in Maurice's reflection? Does one level seem more apt than others to describe Maurice's dilemma with the Pledge of Allegiance?

## REFLECTION AND PEDAGOGICAL CONTENT KNOWLEDGE

Reflection can be a vehicle for transforming what you know about your sub-ject into knowledge of how to teach that subject to students. This kind of knowledge is referred to as *pedagogical content knowledge* (Shulman, 1987). As you begin to think of yourself as a teacher and to gain teaching experience, you need to reflect upon questions such as the following.

- How do you define your subject?
- What are its central concepts and processes?
- How do national and state standards define your content and how you teach it?
- Why should students study your subject?
- Do purposes for teaching your subject differ according to the students you teach?
- What do students need to know and be able to do in your subject area?
- How can you best use curricular materials to support student learning?

- How can you best assess student understanding and proficiency in your subject area?
- What practices and approaches are known to be effective in teaching your subject area?
- What potential misunderstandings about concepts and ideas in your subject might students have?

(Grossman, Schonfeld, & Lee, 2005)

Of course, you will not be able to answer all these questions at this point in your development as a teacher, but if you refer back to this list periodically as you move through your teacher education program, you will see how your pedagogical content knowledge is growing.

### Theory into Practice: Reflecting on Pedagogical Content Knowledge

Elizabeth Lester (a pseudonym) wrote the following reflection during her first year of teaching in a large urban high school. As you read it, consider how Elizabeth combined knowledge of her subject with knowledge of how to teach it in this situation.

**CCSSO Principle 1: Subject Matter Knowledge**

"Sound it ouu . . ." The words escaped my lips before I even knew what I was saying. It was my first month of teaching 9th grade remedial reading, during a frustrating class reading assignment, when I heard myself give the least helpful direction any teacher can give a struggling reader. I felt guilty and chagrined, horrified that my students would think that was all the help I could give them. What would my literacy instructor have thought of me? But then I realized that the students hadn't even noticed—they were used to it. So my student did try to sound it out; for about two seconds he tried. Then he looked up, waiting for me to just say the word for him, a strategy that had worked for him for years without ever helping him grow as a reader.

This was the moment when I realized that I wasn't just lacking experience or expertise in literacy—I knew that. I realized much more profoundly that I had no idea how to teach a child to read . . . I really had no idea how to teach an adolescent disillusioned by years of reading failure to read and understand grade-level material. And here I was, teaching a class for 9th graders with the lowest reading scores in the school. So what was I going to do?

At first I was at a loss as to where to begin—the process of learning to read seemed shrouded in mystery. Doesn't everyone just sort of read? I realized, thankfully, that I didn't have to become a kindergarten or first-grade teacher starting from scratch. I needed to be able to tell what parts of reading my older students could do, and what parts of reading they couldn't do. I realized that I needed to know how to assess my students before I could ever hope to help them with their reading. That's when I decided that seeking out a variety of complementary fluency, vocabulary, phonics, and comprehension assessments was the best way for me to figure out how I could best help my struggling readers. I had to start becoming the reading teacher they needed.

Like many high school English teachers, Elizabeth had excellent content knowledge. She loved literature and was a skilled writer. What she lacked was knowledge of how to transform what she knew about reading into a form (pedagogical content knowledge) that would help her students. Her vignette shows how she begins to develop pedagogical content knowledge by asking herself such questions as:

- What aspects of my subject are most important for my students to learn?
- How do my purposes for teaching change depending on the needs of the student I teach?
- How can I use instruction to support the development of my students' reading proficiency?
- How can I use assessment to gather information about my students' understanding of and proficiency in reading?

As a reflective practitioner, Elizabeth was committed to seeking out, developing, and continually refining practices that addressed the needs of her students. Before her first year of teaching had ended, Elizabeth had researched a variety of sources to design a classroom-based reading portfolio assessment that would enable her to diagnose students' reading difficulties and provide appropriate support for them.

## REFLECTION IN AN ERA OF
## STANDARDS AND ACCOUNTABILITY

Progress has been made in enhancing school success for children and young adults of traditional minority groups, as well as for females, students with exceptionalities, and others. Nevertheless, an achievement gap persists. African Americans, Hispanics, and Native Americans lag behind Whites on many measures of school performance, drop out of school at higher rates, and engage in risky behaviors more frequently. Gender gaps persist in a variety of school subjects. Over the last 2 decades, one way policymakers have sought to close such gaps is through the tools of standards and accountability.

Initially, standards–clear statements of what students should know and be able to do at various levels of schooling–were intended to level the playing field for students who had traditionally been unsuc-

| CCSSO Principle 3: |
| Teaching Diverse |
| Learners |

cessful by making expectations for learning clear to all audiences. Some advocates saw standards as a Bill of Rights for students. For example, if a standard for English language arts stated that students should read a wide variety of texts, but a school did not provide students with a wide variety of texts, then students and their advocates would have firm ground on which to argue for the purchase of more library books.

Policymakers foresaw that standards would have no teeth without accountability. That is, why set goals if there are no consequences for not meeting them? Thus, accountability is present to some degree at every level of education today: The majority of public school students today live in states with exit exam requirements; teacher education programs must provide evidence to the public that the courses and experiences they offer meet standards; and teachers must pass standardized tests in order to be licensed.

The Interstate New Teacher Assessment and Support Consortium (INTASC), a project of the Council of Chief State School Officers (1996), has developed a set of 10 standards, which they refer to as principles, for beginning teacher licensing, assessment, and development. This document identifies the knowledge, skills, and dispositions preservice teachers should exhibit in order to meet each standard. For the purpose of accountability, the Educational Testing Service has developed tests to determine whether aspiring and beginning teachers can meet these standards. The tests are called the Praxis Series™ (based on the Greek word for the practice of an art, science, or skill). Many states now require preservice teachers to take and attain certain scores on various forms of the Praxis test series. These tests measure basic skills in reading, writing, and math, subject matter knowledge; and pedagogical knowledge (Educational Testing Service, 2004).

If standards present clear targets and tests measure the extent to which students and teachers are hitting these targets, why should current and prospective educators ponder their own educational experiences and life stories, welcome uncertainty as an opportunity for inquiry, weigh competing claims and viewpoints, question the political and social implications of schooling? Is reflection even necessary in such an educational climate?

We believe that standards and testing make it more important than ever that teachers be reflective practitioners. Reflection tells us whether the targets that have been set for us are worthy ones. Reflection teaches us how to aim our instruction so that our students will be able not only to demonstrate that they can meet academic standards but also that they can achieve life goals. Through reflection, Ella, Kate, Maurice, and Elizabeth gained important insights that made them better teachers of all students. Standards may be the targets, but reflection guides the arrows.

## SUMMARY

Good teachers are reflective practitioners who know themselves, their students, their subject, and how to teach it. Your self is the first and most important context of teaching. In order to know yourself, it is important to reflect upon your own autobiography and how it will affect your practice. Among the key points to remember are:

- Reflection is a particular type of thinking that encompasses self-assessment, problem-solving, and critical thinking.
- Teaching is part science and part art. Because teachers regularly face complex and uncertain situations, they need to be reflective practitioners.
- Teachers who are reflective practitioners continually seek out, develop, and refine practices that address individual needs and cultural characteristics of students.
- Reflection is one method for developing pedagogical content knowledge—the knowledge of how to teach one's subject to students.
- The standards and accountability movement is in part a response to persistent achievement gaps in education. Today, teachers must demonstrate that they possess the knowledge and skills to be effective in the classroom.
- In an era of standards and accountability, it is imperative that teachers be reflective practitioners so that they can make wise, equitable, and effective decisions about their own and their students' learning.

### *Reflecting on the Standards*

- To what extent would you characterize yourself as a reflective person?
- In what areas of your life has reflection (evaluating the effects of your choices and actions on others) been useful to you?

- Have you ever critiqued your own or someone else's performance? Has anyone ever critiqued your performance? What did you learn from these experiences?
- What do you see as the pros and cons of setting standards for teaching?

# CHAPTER 2

# Knowing Middle and High School Students

Knowledge of who our students are cannot be separated from knowledge of how to teach them. In this chapter, we highlight selected characteristics of the students you will someday teach, confident that as you progress in your career you will make studying your students a lifelong commitment.

The overall purpose of this chapter is related to CCSSO Principle #3: *The teacher understands how students differ in their approaches to learning and creates instructional opportunities that are adapted to diverse learners.*

Specifically, this chapter will help you:

- Recognize how students' learning is influenced by individual experiences, talents, and prior learning as well as language, culture, family, and community values;
- Reflect upon important features of identity that affect how students experience school and how teachers experience students;
- Identify differences in learning styles and intelligences;
- Create equitable learning environments in which individual differences are respected.

Despite the good intentions of teacher educators and teachers themselves, research continues to document disparities in achievement among various groups of students and inequities in their treatment in the curriculum and in teacher-student interaction (Garcia & Guerra, 2004). This makes it imperative that we become aware of factors that may influence our treatment of students and reflect on how our own experiences may have shaped who we are today and what we do in the classroom (Gay & Kirkland, 2003).

## REFLECTING ON PRACTICE:
## LIZ SPALDING–"FROM BEING SMART TO BEING COOL"

For 6 years, I had distinguished myself as an outstanding student at the small Catholic elementary school I attended. I was a happy, high-achieving, husky girl. All that changed when I entered adolescence.

Seventh grade was a miserable year, as I learned that being popular and slim was far more desirable than being smart and chubby. I often came home in tears from being called "fatso," "tub," or "brain." So I studied the popular girls and boys in the class and determined what I needed to do: I lost weight, ditched the lunch box, learned to dance, and started smoking. In class, I quit volunteering and even managed to get punished occasionally.

By the time I entered high school, I had made the transition to cool. My highest priority was popularity. I still did well in my classes, but I carefully avoided being singled out for academic accomplishments. Toward the end of our high school years, most of my classmates and I took the Scholastic Aptitude Test (SAT) for college entrance. Some weeks later, I was horrified to walk into the main lobby of the high school and see my SAT score posted prominently on the main bulletin board. I had performed extremely well on the verbal portion of the test. As I stood there, a male classmate approached, looked at the posted scores, and exclaimed, "God, Spalding! I didn't know you were smart!" I took Bobby's remark as both a compliment and a curse: Apparently I had truly succeeded in my quest to be cool, but I feared that I would now be unmasked as a brain and therefore uncool.

These experiences as a student continue to affect my teaching. I constantly remind myself that what I have to teach is probably *not* the number-one item on my college students' agendas–personal and social goals often take priority over academic ones. Students act as they do for a variety of reasons that may have little to do with your or my teaching. When I was a high school teacher, I had extremely bright students who cheated on vocabulary tests in order to be seen as cool. Recently when a lovely 1st-year high school teacher showed me a note she had intercepted depicting her as an ugly hag, I tried to console her by reminding her that it's just not cool to admit you think your teacher is pretty! As teachers, we must never underestimate the importance of being cool for adolescents.

### Questions to Consider

- What kind of student were you in elementary school, middle school, and high school?
- How did features such as gender, ethnicity, culture, language, religion, or socioeconomic class influence who you were as a student and who your friends were?

- Did you ever feel "different"? Why? How did you treat others whom you perceived as different?

## SOCIETAL CHANGES AFFECTING ADOLESCENTS

Many factors in society influence students' lives and consequently their performance at school. Researchers have been tracking health trends and race/ethnic disparities from adolescent to young adulthood. They have looked at such health indicators as diet, inactivity, obesity, tobacco use, substance abuse, binge drinking, violence, sexually transmitted diseases, mental health, and health care access. They have found that health risk increased and access to health care decreased from the teen to adult years of most U.S. race/ethnic groups, with Native American youth at the highest risk (Harris, Gordon-Larsen, Chantala, & Udry, 2006).

> **CCSSO Principle 2: Learning and Human Development**

Poverty is the greatest of all risk conditions. One quarter of all U.S. children under age 6 live in poverty. Poor children as a group are more likely to be ill or underweight, fall behind or drop out of school, become teen parents, experience economic troubles as adults, and become victims or perpetrators of crimes. Harold Hodgkinson (2003), a demographer and advocate of early intervention in the lives of poor children, concluded that one-third of children born in 2000 were born "highly favored." Another one-third were born into poverty, their life chances severely compromised by an accident of birth.

Violence and drugs continue to invade schools. School shootings in disparate parts of the country have shocked the nation and caused everyone to wonder how such seriously disturbed youth can pass through the school system apparently unnoticed. Indeed, a small but disturbing number of high school students have reported being threatened or injured with a weapon or carrying a weapon (http://www.safeyouth.org).

No one really knows how many youth are affected by trends in immigration and migration. In 2003, 706,000 immigrants were granted legal permanent resident status. Forty percent of these immigrants came from Mexico, India, the Philippines, China, and El Salvador. While their most frequent destinations were California, New York, Texas, Florida, New Jersey, and Illinois; Lincoln, Nebraska has become one of the top 20 cities for new immigrants, its non-White population growing by 128% since 1990 (http://www.dhs.gov/ximgtn/statistics/). At the same time, Americans have the highest known migration rate in the world. Forty-three million move each year, and low-income children move more often than middle-income kids. Teachers who teach in high-mobility areas often end the school year with class rosters that only vaguely resemble the rosters with which they began the year (Hodginkson, 2003).

Even if you plan to teach in the community where you grew up, it may no longer be the *same* community where you grew up. Communities are rapidly changing as new residents move in and other residents move on.

## GOOD NEWS ABOUT ADOLESCENTS

One has to do a bit of searching to find good news about adolescents. But it's there if you look for it. For example, there are many indications that student academic performance is improving, not declining, and that more and more students are enrolling in and completing rigorous courses in high school (Viadero, 2004). In both curricular and extracurricular areas, middle and high school students are making a difference in their communities and acting as responsible citizens. As schools, classes, and individuals they are standing up to racism, social injustice, degradation of the environment, and homophobia (Fossey, 2008; Townsend, 2001; http://www.whatkidscando.org).

Unless we interact with them daily, we rarely hear the voices of the many adolescents who invest themselves in their school experiences, have faith in their teachers to guide them in their learning, and believe that education will not only help them fulfill their dreams for the future, but also has value in the here and now.

## SOCIOCULTURAL CHARACTERISTICS OF ADOLESCENTS

Gender, race, ethnicity, language, culture, socioeconomic status, and religion are known as sociocultural characteristics because they are not simply biological features or financial statistics, but are given

CCSSO Principle 2: Learning and Human Development

meanings by the larger society (socio) and culture (cultural) in which they exist. More important, consequences result from the meanings given by society. Gender, for example, is not simply a biological feature. It carries with it definite societal expectations for girls and boys. A walk down the toy aisles of any retail store should illustrate this clearly. In some parts of the United States, a person who speaks with a Southern accent may be looked upon as ignorant, even if she has a law degree from Yale. Fashion-conscious teens whose parents earn high incomes may snub other teens based on the labels on their clothing.

## Gender and Sexual Orientation

In order for you to know your students and teach them well, you need to consider how gender and sexual orientation influence what goes on in schools and classrooms and how you can create a safe and equitable learning environment for all students. Research continues to document that schools differentiate between males and females, and between heterosexual and homosexual orientations to the disadvantage of all (Klein, 2007).

While females choose math/science careers in disproportionately lower numbers than males (Xie & Shauman, 2003), it appears that male academic performance overall lags behind that of females. Gender equity is a persistent problem. Both boys and girls suffer from sexual harassment and stereotyping into gender roles. Teachers continue to focus more classroom attention on boys. A gender gap is opening up in technology, as boys enter school with more computer experience than girls (Sadker, 2000).

A recent poll revealed that approximately 750,000 students nationwide identify as gay or lesbian (http://www.glsen.org). This figure implies that there is at least one gay or lesbian student in every middle and high school classroom and that the majority of middle and high school students know at least one person (a friend or family member) who is gay or lesbian. In addition, some adolescents discover that their orientation is bisexual or that they identify most closely with the opposite gender (transgender). Students such as those described above are often referred to under the umbrella term of LGBT (lesbian, gay, bisexual, transgender). LGBT students need supportive and accepting teachers as much as, if not more than, heterosexual students of any ethnic or socioeconomic group (Ressler & Chase, 2009).

## Race

The usefulness of race as a way to categorize human beings is called into question if we look at the increasing diversity of our society (Hollingshead, 1995). Despite this fact, the United States remains a race-conscious society (Bennett, 2006). Just as we notice whether our students are male or female, whether they are short or tall, we notice the physical characteristics that imply race. It is neither honest nor helpful for teachers to claim to be color-blind. In fact, this claim implies that difference in skin color is a disadvantage to be minimized. Furthermore, for many students race is an essential aspect of their identity that requires recognition and affirmation (Nieto, 2003).

> **CCSSO Principle 2:**
> **Learning and**
> **Human Development**

## Ethnicity

Banks (1994) defines an ethnic group as "a group that shares a common ancestry, culture, history, tradition, and sense of peoplehood" (p. 91). For example, the U.S. Census applies the racial category of Hispanic to people whose ethnic heritage may be Mexican, Salvadoran, Puerto Rican, Dominican, or Guatemalan. Similarly, there are countless White ethnic groups within our country: Polish, Irish, Italian, and German Americans. Ethnicity, like race, is an important aspect of identity (Peshkin, 1991).

## Culture

Sonia Nieto has defined culture as:

The ever-changing values, traditions, social and political relationships, and worldview created and shared by a group of people bound together by a combination of factors (which can include a common history, geographic location, language, social class, and/or religion) and how these are transformed by those who share them. (2003, p. 390)

Culture is such a deeply ingrained part of who we are that it is often invisible to us, leading us to believe that the way we think and behave is the right and natural way.

When the culture in the home or community differs from the culture of the school, cultural conflicts can occur. These conflicts may spring from differences in verbal and nonverbal communication styles, the organization of time, the organization of space, and a number of other factors. Cultural conflicts are often attributed to differences in race or ethnicity and the accompanying differences in worldview (Delpit, 1995).

## Language

Language is a particularly salient manifestation of culture and a deeply ingrained aspect of identity. In 2001–2002, a survey conducted by the U.S. Department of Education identified 4,747,763 students enrolled in public schools as *Limited English Proficient* (LEP). This represents a 95% increase in the number of LEP students since 1991, while the overall school population has increased by only 12%.

> **CCSSO Principle 5: Motivation and Management**

The same survey listed 436 different languages spoken by students. The five most commonly spoken were: Spanish, Vietnamese, Hmong, Chinese, and

Korean (http://www.ed.gov/about/offices/list/ocr/ellresources.html). You can support the learning of linguistically diverse students by showing an interest in and respect for their native languages and cultures and by considering linguistic differences among your students when planning for and implementing instruction.

## Social Groups and Socioeconomic Status (SES)

Student social groups are an enduring and important feature of adolescent life (Brantlinger, 1993). Student decisions about what to wear, with whom to

> **CCSSO Principle 2:**
> **Learning and**
> **Human Development**

socialize, where to spend the lunch period, and even what to eat at lunch are not whimsical or arbitrary: they are the very fabric of student culture.

In a 2-year study of social groups in a large Midwestern suburban high school, Penelope Eckert (1989) found two broad social categories among the students: "jocks" and "burnouts." Whether a student becomes a jock or a burnout is not so much a matter of individual choice as a reflection of the socioeconomic status of one's parents.

In Eckert's (1989) study, jocks were generally children of middle-class status. They embraced the values of the school (e.g., respect for authority, punctuality, orientation toward individual achievement), which were aligned with middle-class values. For them, high school was a good setting in which to practice anticipated adult skills and roles, such as persisting into higher education and seeking white-collar employment.

Burnouts were generally children of working-class status. They were alienated from the school and generally declined to participate in either academic or extracurricular activities. Their behavior was not deviant or delinquent;

> **CCSSO Principle 2:**
> **Learning and**
> **Human Development**

rather, it reflected working-class norms, values, and social relationships. For them, "High school . . . is not simply a bad experience—it teaches them lessons that threaten to limit them for the rest of their lives" (p. 181).

Numerous studies confirm the critical role socioeconomic class plays in students' school success (Fine, Burns, Payne, & Torre, 2004; Kozol, 1991; Oakes, 1985).

## Religion

The principle of separation of church and state is usually attributed to the First Amendment to the U.S. Constitution. In public schools, this principle has played out primarily as a prohibition against requiring students to pray in or out of class and against the promotion of any one denomination or religion at the expense of another (http://www.ReligiousTolerance.org). However, neither teachers nor students leave their religious convictions outside the doors of the school. In addition to being a sociocultural characteristic that carries consequences, religion is a fundamental part of the identity of many people (Williams, 2005) and it affects what is taught and learned in schools. The ongoing battles over the teaching of evolution and censorship of certain books (e.g., the *Harry Potter* series) are just two examples of how religion enters the classroom, whether we wish it to or not. For some students, a deep religious faith is what enables them to survive and rise above poverty (Kozol, 2001).

There is no doubt that public schools are organized around the calendar and values of mainstream American Protestantism. But that particular religious tradition is more problematic than ever before as our society becomes more diverse. One researcher recently identified 10,000 distinct religions in the world (Ostling, 2001) and those religions are showing up in our schools. Today, a diverse public middle or high school may contain mainstream Protestants, evangelical Christians, Roman Catholics, Jews, Latter-day Saints, Buddhists, Hindus, Muslims, Wiccans, and practitioners of other faiths. Within each of these denominations there is diversity as well. The rise of hate crimes against members of some religious groups, especially since September 11, 2001, makes it impossible to ignore the impact of religion on schools.

***Theory into Practice: Reflecting on a Troubled Student.*** Sophia Coronado wrote the following reflection during her 5th year of teaching at a large urban/suburban high school. As you read it, think about the many dimensions along which students differ and how Sophia considered these differences.

> Alan was one of my most likable seniors. He was a gregarious, handsome, well-kept student, with regular attendance and good grades. He always greeted me with a smile and friendly hello, and kept me up-to-date on events in his life. Alan was attentive in class, participated in discussions, and got along well with his peers. I think he particularly enjoyed my English class because his two best friends and his girlfriend were also students in my class. And so, the first 9 weeks of school passed pleasantly.
>
> But then I began to notice a change in Alan's behavior. It was a subtle change, and I noticed his attendance first. He began missing

my class 1 or 2 days a week. Then, Alan was consistently absent at least 3 days a week. And the days he did come to class, he generally came late. He would walk in 10, 15 minutes into my lecture, wearing mismatched clothes and his slippers, looking as if he just rolled out of bed. He would then make his way to his desk, put his head down, and sleep for the remainder of the period. This seemed out of character for Alan, so I tried to teasingly chide him about how I was taking his absence from my class personally. He mumbled something about working late or not feeling well or personal problems, and said he would do better. Concerned, but not wanting to pry, I let it go.

But things only got worse. His high "B" grade began slipping due to his absences and missed assignments. When in attendance, he rarely engaged in discussions and he avoided interaction with others. This once trendily dressed and easygoing young man was now unkempt and at times, surly. As the semester wore on, neither Alan's attendance, grades, or behavior improved.

On the last day of the semester, while waiting to administer the final exam, I noticed Alan enter my room. I was surprised to see him, but thankful he had decided to come to class. While I was talking with another student, Alan engaged in a verbal altercation with one of his best friends. I asked the two to settle down, thinking it was only typical male high school posturing. I turned to resume my conversation with the other student when the situation escalated and Alan physically attacked his friend. Desks were tipped over and punches were flying. I screamed for the young men to separate, but Alan ignored me. He continued to attack his friend. After I called into the hall for campus police, Alan stopped punching the other student and stormed out of the room. Shocked and shaken, I managed to get the class seated and started on the final exam.

Ten minutes later, with campus police searching for him, Alan returned to my classroom and asked if he could talk with me. He was visibly upset and told me how sorry he was to have behaved that way in my classroom, that his life was spiraling out of control, and that he hoped I would forgive him. He admitted that the attack was premeditated and that the situation had been brewing for weeks, all over an incident involving his best friend and his girlfriend. He then hugged me and apologized one more time, before campus police led him away. When he left, I couldn't help feeling that it was Alan who deserved my apology. For weeks I had felt something was wrong, but I never took the time to ask him if he needed help. I couldn't stop thinking that if I had acted upon my intuition, maybe things would have turned out differently.

*Questions to Consider.* The vignette above is rich; yet there is much we do not know about Sophia, Alan, or the situation. Think about the sociocultural characteristics described in this chapter so far. How might any or all of them have played a role in the interactions between Sophia and Alan and in Alan's academic deterioration and meltdown? To what degree might gender have been a factor in this vignette? Is it possible gender influenced Sophia's decision "not to pry," for example? We do not know the race, ethnicity, culture, native language, or religion of either Sophia or Alan. Consider how each of these factors or the interplay of them might have influenced what happened in Sophia's classroom. Might the outcomes for Alan be different depending on whether he is White, African American, Hispanic, middle class, working class? Also consider:

- How does knowing your students help you recognize when they may be troubled?
- As a result of this incident, how do you think Sophia might behave differently in the future?

## EXCEPTIONAL STUDENTS

*Exceptionality* refers to an array of characteristics that qualify individual students to receive special services (Culatta & Tompkins, 1999.) Traditionally, students with exceptionalities have received special services in programs that removed them from the general education classroom. More recently, the trend has been toward inclusion. Many middle and high schools have successfully become inclusive and report that all students benefit, both socially and academically, in an inclusive environment (Burstein, Sears, Wilcoxen, Cabello, & Spagna, 2004).

*Giftedness* also falls under the umbrella of exceptionalities. Proponents of gifted education argue that regular classroom instruction does not meet the special needs of gifted students and that many teachers and students are hostile to gifted students. They make the case that gifted students need to be removed to an environment where they can be with other students like themselves. Proponents of inclusive schools, like Sapon-Shevin (1995), argue that the needs of gifted students should be accommodated in the regular classroom: When students with differences of any sort are removed from the classroom for whatever reason, the whole classroom community is diminished.

## LEARNING STYLES

Learning styles are "the unique ways whereby an individual gathers and processes information and are the means by which an individual prefers to learn" (Davidson, 1990, p. 36). The key words here are *unique* and *prefers.* That is, not every person learns in the same way, and people have different preferences about how to learn best. Numerous learning-style inventories or profiles have been developed. For example, instruments have been developed to determine students' preferences in the areas of cognition, perception, learning environment, social interaction, and physiological factors.

<table>
<tr><td>CCSSO Principle 2:<br>Learning and<br>Human Development</td></tr>
</table>

Proponents of learning-style theory attempt to make teachers aware that: 1. students have different styles of learning; 2. teachers tend to teach according to their own preferred learning styles; 3. school success often hinges upon being able to learn in a single style; and 4. teachers need to vary their instructional styles to address the varied learning styles of their students.

Historically, school has worked best for learners who can think abstractly, logically, and sequentially; who learn well from listening and the written word; who are autonomous and/or easily motivated by authority figures (Shields, 1993). Many students, however, differ from this description. For example, some learners prefer the concrete and immediate to the abstract; some learners think intuitively, imaginatively, or globally; some students need to see, touch, move, or manipulate in order to understand; some students learn best when they receive a lot of feedback from adults and/or can talk to their peers. Such traits sometimes land students in academic or disciplinary difficulty.

Learning-style theory gives teachers another tool for understanding students and determining what kinds of experiences may best help them learn. Learning-style theory allows teachers to view learners as different—not necessarily as slow, bright, motivated, or unmotivated. In addition to planning instruction that reaches students with a variety of learning styles, you can also help students to discover their own styles, capitalize on their strengths, and minimize their weaknesses (Silver, Strong, & Perini, 2000).

## MULTIPLE INTELLIGENCES

Howard Gardner's (1993, 1999) theory of multiple intelligences gives educators a soundly researched and scrupulously documented means to identify and describe the many ways in which people are intelligent. Prior to the publication of Gardner's theory, it was widely assumed that intelligence could be determined through a pen-and-pencil test and translated into a single number that remained more or less constant throughout life. IQ was closely linked to school success, and this was not surprising because both instruction and assessment in schools generally focused on verbal, mathematical, and logical skills.

Applying rigorous qualifying criteria and using examples of historical and contemporary geniuses from this culture and others, Gardner has identified eight intelligences: linguistic, musical, logical/mathematical, spatial, bodily-kinesthetic, intrapersonal, interpersonal, and naturalistic. These eight are briefly described in Table 2.1.

Intelligences overlap and a person may be gifted in more than one intelligence. For example, Tiger Woods appears to have intrapersonal and interpersonal gifts as well as bodily-kinesthetic intelligence. Gardner's theory was not intended for use in simplistically labeling students. Rather, it offers teachers another important lens for viewing diversity in the classroom (Armstrong, 1994).

## CREATING EQUITABLE LEARNING ENVIRONMENTS

All human beings have more similarities than differences. Recognizing and building upon our similarities enable us to form communities in the classroom and in the world, sharing common values and goals. At the same time, we must respond to individual and group differences within communities in order to ensure that all members have equal opportunities to participate in the life of the community.

**CCSSO Principle 5: Motivation and Management**

Creating an equitable learning environment may require that you treat students differently according to relevant differences. Below are some guidelines to consider.

- Hold high expectations for educational attainment for every student.
- Critically examine your own beliefs about who can learn.
- Affirm diversity as a value, not a deficit.
- Integrate students' life experiences into the learning process.
- Engage students as active participants in instruction.
- Use a wide variety of grouping practices to give students experience working in a variety of group configurations including large, small, heterogeneous, and cooperative teams.
- Physically organize the classroom for diversity, including attention to classroom decor and to the arrangement of furniture and equipment.
- Collaborate with families and communities to make instruction more meaningful (Garcia & Guerra, 2004; Stainback, Stainback, & Slavin, 1989).

**TABLE 2.1. Gardner's Multiple Intelligences**

| Intelligence | Description | Sample Activities |
|---|---|---|
| Verbal/ Linguistic | Reading, writing, speaking, and listening in one's own or a foreign language | Reading books<br>Playing word, board, or card games<br>Listening to recordings<br>Participating in conversations and discussions |
| Logical/ Mathematical | Number and computing skills, recognizing patterns and relationships, the ability to solve problems through logic | Classifying and sequencing<br>Playing number and logic games<br>Solving puzzles and riddles |
| Visual/ Spatial | Visual perception of environment, ability to create and manipulate mental images and to orient the body in space | Using graphic and plastic arts<br>Observing<br>Solving mazes and other spatial tasks<br>Exercises in imagery and imagination |
| Bodily/ Kinesthetic | Physical coordination and dexterity, using fine- and gross-motor skills, and expressing oneself through physical activity | Playing with blocks and other construction materials<br>Dancing<br>Playing sports and games<br>Acting in plays and make-believe<br>Using manipulatives to solve problems |
| Musical | Understanding and expressing oneself through music and rhythm or dance | Listening to recordings<br>Engaging in rhythmic games and activities<br>Singing and dancing<br>Playing musical instruments |
| Interpersonal | Understanding how to communicate with and understand other people | Group projects and discussions<br>Cooperative games<br>Multicultural books and materials<br>Dramatic activities |
| Intrapersonal | Understanding one's inner world of emotions and thoughts | Independent projects<br>Journaling<br>Finding quiet spaces for reflection<br>Imaginative activities and games |
| Naturalist | Understanding the world of plants and animals | Explore nature<br>Collect, study, and group objects<br>Care for plants and animals |

Adapted from Dickinson, 1996.

What other ways can you think of for making your classroom equitable and inclusive?

## SUMMARY

Schools and teachers can and should take an active role in fostering respect for differences and in using diversity as a resource for curriculum and instruction. Among the key points to remember are:

- Sociocultural characteristics of adolescents have a great deal to do with how they perceive schools and teachers, how teachers interact with them, and whether or not they will conclude that school success is a worthy goal.
- Learning styles, multiple intelligences, and exceptionalities are among the variables that affect student learning and performance.
- Diversity among today's students challenges teachers to break out of the old mold of "one-size-fits-all" instruction and to move toward creating equitable and inclusive learning communities.

As the case of Sophia and Alan suggests, diversity manifests itself in classrooms in unpredictable ways. Knowing your students will help you make the most of their strengths and deal effectively with their slumps. A single teacher, a single class, or even a single learning experience can change the course of a student's life.

### *Reflecting on the Standards*

- What does an equitable learning environment in your subject area look like?
- How can you help students with differing personal and family backgrounds and various skills, talents, and interests make connections to your subject area?
- Do you agree that all students can learn at high levels? Why or why not?
- What should be the influence of community and cultural norms in your classroom?
- Are there groups or students with individual differences that you will need to make a special effort to reach?

# Part II

# CLASSROOM CONTEXTS OF TEACHING

# CHAPTER 3

# Rethinking Classroom Management

For every teacher there is a beginning, just as there was for the authors when we began teaching in our early twenties. Often the decision to become a teacher is based on some altruistic notion—because we love kids, because we want to contribute to society, because we feel called to the teaching profession even though we know that teacher salaries are lower than for other, more prestigious professions. Regardless of why a person chooses a teaching career, all beginning teachers share one challenge: facing the daunting responsibility of motivating students into becoming a community of learners characterized by positive social interaction and active engagement.

The overall purpose of this chapter is related to CCSSO Principle #5: *The teacher uses an understanding of individual and group motivation and behavior to create a learning environment that encourages positive social interaction, active engagement in learning, and self-motivation.*

Specifically, this chapter will help you:

- Use the resources of time, space, and activities to engage students in learning;
- Explore factors in establishing a learning community where, with your guidance, students assume increasing responsibility for themselves and one another, make decisions, and work productively both collaboratively and independently;
- Consider a classroom management style that promotes intrinsic motivation by helping students see lessons as personally relevant, allowing them to make choices in their learning, and leading them to ask questions and solve problems whether academic or social;
- Reflect on classroom management practices you experienced in school and think more broadly and critically about conventional approaches.

## *REFLECTING ON PRACTICE:*
## JOSEPH BRAUN–"MANAGING MORE THAN MISCONDUCT"

On my first day as a teacher, I stepped into the classroom aware that my dream of becoming a teacher was now a reality. That thought was so unbelievably scary, and at the same time so incredibly exciting, that I wasn't sure if I could even get through the first day. I felt clumsy, shy, and unsure of myself as a teacher. But I did get through that day, and many more, with the days eventually turning into years.

I began my teaching with a commitment to avoid using fear and power as a way to control students; instead I would focus on trying to keep students interested and engaged by relating lessons to students personal interests and clearly communicating expectations and processes for communication. A great idea, but in practice sometimes I was more successful than other times.

Since I was a beginning teacher, the principal assigned me a mentor, Mr. Mortenson, a veteran teacher with over 25 years of experience. From him, I received an on-the-job crash course in many practical dimensions of classroom management. Mr. Mortenson clarified my initial confusion by explaining that student discipline is just one subset of the bigger and broader notion of classroom management. *Student discipline* is managing student behavior in effective, respectful, and trustful ways. *Classroom management* refers to the ways in which a teacher organizes the classroom environment, such as time, resources, and space, so the students can work together cooperatively on worthwhile academic activities, culminating in assessing and communicating what is learned. These activities are continuous, engaging, and culturally sensitive. As my first year of teaching drew to a close, I couldn't thank Mr. Mortenson enough for what he taught me.

### Questions to Consider

- What are some practices that you have encountered that you would use or not use as part of your classroom management and student discipline routines?
- How are the managerial tasks described above similar to or different from the tasks performed by managers in other professions (e.g., sports, entertainment, business, industry)?

## TOWARD GREATER AWARENESS
## OF CLASSROOM MANAGEMENT

Today, most teacher education programs introduce the dynamics of classroom management well in advance of student teaching. Beginning with readings and followed by classroom observations or field-based research projects, many preservice teachers have ample opportunities to explore the many facets of classroom management prior to crossing that classroom threshold as a student teacher. No program, however, could teach you all you need to know about classroom management, and very few teachers manage classrooms well on the first day they begin teaching: Expertise in management improves with time, experience, reflection, and effective mentoring.

One way to begin thinking about classroom management is to view yourself as a relationship specialist (Kottler, Zehm, & Kottler, 2005). When you assume this role, you begin to notice how the relationships you form with students influence the tone and demeanor of your classroom. You will also explore your personal predispositions for interpersonal relationships and gauge how well they align with (or misalign with) those of your students. In this sense, managing a classroom is not about controlling or dominating students, nor is it owning students for the short time you have them in your classroom. Rather, managing becomes a process of negotiating space, listening to others, and understanding and affirming needs.

## EASING CONCERNS ABOUT CLASSROOM MANAGEMENT

Placing classroom management in proper perspective may help alleviate some of your concerns. Most of the challenges you will face relative to classroom management and student discipline will not be serious ones, although they might seem to be when you first interact with students. The most common management challenges you will face will be minor distractions, and because most teachers are innovators (and you will become one, too), you will quickly learn how to deal with these kinds of events without major disruptions to classroom instruction.

This is not to say that more serious classroom management and student misbehavior problems will not occur. In some schools, students seem unable to control their anger or to resolve conflicts peaceably and bring the stress and violence they experience in the world beyond into the classroom. Some seem to abide by no linguistic or social taboos. Some students carry weapons to school, while others have drugs in their possession. Such violent and destructive behaviors make managing classrooms more challenging than it has ever been. But be assured that where these more serious situations exist, they do not occur all the time, and in many schools they do not occur at all.

## TOWARD SUCCESSFUL CLASSROOM MANAGEMENT

This section focuses on the key elements needed for effective classroom management by addressing the following question: Does your organization, allocation, and management of the resources of time, space, physical materials, activities, and attention provide active and equitable engagement of students in productive tasks? Elements that address this question are organized into four clusters: practical, cultural, metaphorical, and personal.

## Practical Elements

Beginning teachers typically face these questions: How do I set up my classroom instruction? How much time do I allow for specific activities? What materials should I use? How closely do I need to adhere to the district's prescribed curriculum? How much should the cultural backgrounds of my students influence what and how I teach? Should I put my desks in straight rows or in clusters? Under what circumstances should I send disruptive students to the principal's office and when should I deal with them myself?

Each of the above questions, like so many others, can be answered with the same ambiguous response: "It depends." The *it depends* phenomenon becomes especially apparent when you speak with experienced teachers. For example, how you set up your classroom depends on the culture of the school where you teach, the content, and the needs of students. How much time you allow for an activity depends on the nature of the activity, what is to be learned, where it takes place, and the abilities of the students to engage in it. Sending disruptive students to the office depends on school policy, the nature of the student misbehavior, and the views you hold of classroom management and student discipline.

There are many variables to consider when you begin organizing a management plan, and there are even more to consider when you actually implement it. To help you consider the practical dimensions of classroom management, we provide you with descriptions of selected areas.

***Thinking About Classroom Space and Tone.*** The physical environment of your classroom is the actual classroom setting: desk arrangement, placement of teacher's desk, storage room for teaching materials, and so on. When you set up your physical environment and express your own personality in this environment, another important dimension of the environment emerges—the *tone* of your classroom. Tone is how your classroom feels to your students as they interact with you, peers, and the prescribed curriculum. If the tone helps students feel comfortable, needed, and valued, then students will be more engaged in learning.

When you take a step back to appraise your classroom space and attempt to gain a sense of the classroom tone, think about these questions:

- Have I established a positive climate for students?
- Are students treated equitably regardless of their background, academic strengths and weaknesses, or cultural heritage?
- What accommodations for students with special needs need to be made?
- Where is the best place to store learning materials, such as computers and other AV equipment, so they are accessible yet not in the way?
- How can I make the classroom comfortable and an engaging and challenging learning environment for my students, e.g. by decorating classroom walls with posters, pictures, and student work?

***Thinking About Time.*** The school day in most middle and high schools is divided into blocks of time. It usually begins and ends with ringing bells, and you become attuned to a life of seconds, minutes, and hours. How you use the time allotted for each class reflects your ability to plan effectively and carry out meaningful learning experiences. Effective classroom managers know how to use every moment of classroom time for learning activities.

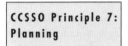

CCSSO Principle 7: Planning

Central to managing time effectively is thinking about the time spent on instructional and noninstructional activities. Noninstructional activities include tasks such as taking attendance or returning graded papers. Little or no instruction occurs unless you have planned for it in advance by having students engaged productively in learning while these tasks are completed. Your goal should be to spend as little time as possible on noninstructional activities, thereby providing greater opportunities for meaningful learning experiences.

The following questions are intended to help you think more broadly about time management:

- When involved in administrative duties, what should I have students do that engages them in the daily instruction?
- How can I move from one instructional activity to another and minimize off-task behavior?
- What kind of pace do I establish for the lesson?
- What should I do when some students finish an assignment earlier than other students?
- How much time should I spend giving students individual assistance on independent assignments versus group work while allowing for full and varied participation of all individuals?

***Thinking About Learning Experiences.*** Learning experiences occur when students are formally engaged in an instructional activity for the purpose of acquiring or applying knowledge, skills, or disposi-

| CCSSO Principle 3: |
| Adapting |
| Instruction |

tions. As you begin to think about learning experiences, consider the diversity among your students and the content they are expected to learn. For example, if you are planning a field trip, what accommodations will you need to make for students with special needs? If you are having a guest speaker, what social skills will you need to review with students prior to the guest's arrival? How long can you reasonably expect 13-year-olds to work quietly and independently in their seats?

***Thinking About Routines.*** Setting up clear and predictable classroom routines makes classroom management so much easier. Routines are among the most important features of your classroom. This is because routines let students know what is expected–when they should perform certain tasks and how learning experiences are structured. Successful teachers learn how to connect routines, learning experiences, and content to be taught so that the classroom runs smoothly, with clear expectations and direction.

***Thinking About How You Communicate with Students.*** Jacob Kounin (1977) coined the term "withitness" to describe how aware a teacher is of

| CCSSO Principle 6: |
| Communication |

what is going on in the classroom. This is the key to when and how you communicate with students regarding what they are (or are not) doing. You may not know everything going on in the classroom, but you must communicate to students an attitude that says you do. Proximity control, how close you are physically to a student, is an important nonverbal form of communication, as are voice tone, eye contact, and body language. Active listening–paraphrasing what another is saying as a way of checking for understanding and encouraging the person to continue expressing herself–is an important communication strategy teachers can use (Gordon, 1974).

***Thinking About Relationships with Students.*** The relationships you develop with students are vitally important to their willingness to learn. Reflect for a moment on three of your middle and high school teachers. The first teacher you think about should be one of your favorites, someone whose footsteps you would like to follow, a role model. The second teacher should be someone who has one or two qualities you admire and are considering incorporating into your teaching style. The third teacher should be someone who was not helpful to you and has few qualities you admire. Think about the relationships each of these teachers had with their students. How would you describe these relationships? Educational? Friendly? Warm? Close? Respectful? Distant? Cold? Professional? Helpful? Sensitive?

As you reflect on these teachers, consider how their relationships with students influenced the climates of their classrooms. Think also about their routines and the learning you experienced. Given the teachers' relationships with students and the routines and learning experiences they developed, how would you describe their classroom management? How did they address student discipline problems?

***Thinking About Student Discipline.*** Few topics concern beginning teachers more than student discipline (Meister & Melnick, 2004). In fact, student discipline is such an overpowering concern that many novice teachers think it is synonymous with classroom management. But discipline is only one subset of classroom management—the subset addressing student behavior, and the subset that challenges every educator on almost every day of professional life.

Academic theory about student discipline consists of principles that can be quite helpful when considering generalizable approaches to student behavior. Generalizable approaches are presumed to work with most students in most classrooms most of the time, regardless of local variations in school, classroom, or student cultures. Books discussing the various academic theories of student discipline abound, and many present selected academic theories of student discipline in a single volume, making it convenient to compare and contrast various theories (see Charles & Senter, 2004; Edwards, 2003; Tauber, 2007).

Table 3.1 gives an overview of the range of ideas of some of today's most widely used models. This figure places five academic theories of discipline on a continuum that ranges from student-centered to teacher-centered. Another way of arranging the theories might be from *controlling* student behavior to *influencing* student behavior (Tauber, 2007). If you read each column, you will understand in general terms each theorist's approach to changing student behavior. Reading across each row, you can identify the principles, goals, and strategies that most align with your current beliefs about discipline.

Not surprisingly, each theory has adherents, and some schools have even adopted a single model, such as Assertive Discipline, to be applied consistently by all teachers. More commonly, however, teachers use an eclectic approach to student discipline, taking bits and pieces of academic theories and mixing them with their own personal, practical theories for student discipline.

Ultimately, discipline involves a teacher's understanding of how social groups function and influence people, and how people influence groups. For example, if an individual has a high need to control others, his interactions

**TABLE 3.1. Academic Theories of Discipline**

| Theory/Model | Behavior Modification/ Assertive Discipline | Classroom Climate | Reality Therapy/ Control Theory | Teacher Effectiveness Training | Just Community |
|---|---|---|---|---|---|
| Theoretical Tenets | The teacher systematically uses rewards and punishments to shape and maintain behavior | To establish a positive classroom climate through teacher-student relationship | Having autonomy as a student increases the control and self-esteem in a student's life | Teacher and student use a conflict resolution strategy | Teachers and students use democratic processes to continually develop community norms |
| Names Associated with Theory/ Model | B. F. Skinner  Lee Cantor | Driekurs, Ginott, Kounin, Curwin Mueller | William Glasser | Thomas Gordon | Lawrence Kohlberg |
| Implementation Strategies | Teacher uses rewards and punishment to control students' behavior. Rewards might involve special recognition or privilege. | Teacher's "withitness" critical: voice tone, body language, communication skills, respect for students build positive relationships | Classroom meetings/ contracts can help students make good choices by making clear the connection between student behavior and its consequences | Uses a "no-lose" method of conflict resolution to address problems along with "active listening" to facilitate communication | The "just community" is a forum for discussing and dealing with problems emerging from life in the classroom |
| Pitfalls or problems | Does not develop self-discipline and when rewards cease desired behaviors dwindle away | Not always easy to maintain given the pace of classroom interactions | Takes considerable classroom time and prior training to implement successfully | Not easy to implement given the differences in rates of student development and growth | Teachers need to facilitate group process but not relinquish total authority |

with a group would be significantly different from how someone who easily gives over control to others and goes along with the crowd interacts with a group. Discipline includes how teachers work with these dynamics. Thus, becoming familiar with the theories of discipline described above, and how they can be implemented successfully with most classes, is invaluable in building a foundation to your discipline plan. It is also a good idea to talk to experienced, effective teachers. Their personal, practical theories are important sources of information about student discipline. Listening to their comments and comparing and contrasting their personal theories can also be helpful.

## Cultural Elements of Classroom Management

A sound classroom management plan considers cultural elements. In this section, we describe two cultural elements that influence your management practices: 1. multiple forms of diversity students express in your classes and in their home communities and 2. early adolescent (middle school) and later adolescent (high school) cultures and needs.

*Thinking About Diversity Among Students.* Over the past few decades, society has become more sensitive to all forms of diversity, a trend that increasingly manifests itself in schools and classrooms. This has occurred for several reasons. One, America's shifting demographics are reshaping school populations everywhere. A second reason is the growing movement toward educational egalitarianism. A continuation of the Civil Rights movement of the 1960s, educational egalitarianism aligns with the premise that all students should have an engaging and challenging school learning environment. Consistent with this movement is the reality that students who were once marginalized in schools are no longer passive toward being silenced, nor are they complacent about curriculum and instruction that may be misaligned with their cultural and personal ways of knowing (Greene, 1993).

> **CCSSO Principle 3: Adapting Instruction**

Diversity poses important challenges for teachers. Perhaps the most important is managing classroom learning environments in such a way that all students, not just those who comprise the mainstream culture, are engaged in meaningful learning experiences. When you reflect on the needs of all students, you may begin to appreciate why it may not be educationally sound or even possible to implement in its entirety any of the generalizable academic theories discussed earlier. Diversity is a critical reason to pause and think more deeply about how academic theories and management strategies align with your students.

> **CCSSO Principle 2: Learning and Human Development**

*Thinking About Middle and High School Cultures.* Greater attention has been given recently to distinguishing between the developmental needs of 10- to 14- and 15- to 18-year-olds (Stevenson, 2002). Out of this concern emerged the middle school movement, an attempt to provide early adolescents with models of schooling that meet their developmental needs.

Consider the following description of the developmental tasks of adolescents:

- Moving toward independence from parents, siblings, and childhood friends while retaining significant and enduring ties.
- Developing increasing autonomy in making personal decisions.
- Establishing new friendships.
- Moving toward greater personal intimacy and adult sexuality.
- Dealing with more complex intellectual challenges (Caskey & Anfara, 2007).

This list has many implications for managing middle school classrooms. Some sixth graders, for example, have difficulty just staying seated for an extended period of time. Some may look like children, while others exhibit all the physical characteristics of older teens. How can you, as a prospective middle school teacher, provide a classroom environment that helps early adolescents move toward independence and autonomy, but at the same time provide the structure and support they need as they learn to exercise these skills? What kind of a classroom environment will address students' needs to establish new friendships yet retain important ties with significant adults (including you)?

Compelling evidence suggests that older adolescents need the attention of caring adults no less than younger adolescents. Many are motivated by the belief that they will be able to make important contributions as adults. Nearly all high school juniors and seniors have the full array of cognitive tools and the capacity to learn, but too many have not acquired academic tools for a combination of reasons. Nevertheless, almost all students share a need to be special and desire recognition and help with the journey to adulthood (Pruitt, 2000).

In addition to developmental needs, all people share interpersonal needs. These four interpersonal needs we call the four A's of life, because they are with us across all levels of human development from infancy to old age. These four interpersonal needs are for *attention, acceptance, approval,* and *affection.* In essence these 4 A's of life are the things people seek from family and relationships with others. When unfilled, students may turn to undesirable ways to get these needs met. For example, gang membership is a potent source of attention, affection, acceptance, and approval within the gang culture.

The extent to which a school culture recognizes students' developmental and interpersonal needs will be a measure of its success. The smaller and more personalized learning communities that middle schools and some high schools are embracing are significant shifts in school culture overall. Schools are making these changes as ways of accommodating and meeting the unique developmental needs of adolescents as well as the interpersonal ones.

## Metaphorical Elements of Classroom Management

A metaphor is a type of comparison, but it does not use the words *like* or *as.* When we make statements like, "Alice is a wizard with computers," or "War is hell," or "Love is a rose," we do not literally mean, for example, that Alice has magical powers. Rather, we are making an imaginative comparison. Examining the metaphors we often take for granted in our thinking and in our speech can help us see things in a new light (Lakoff & Johnson, 1980).

Think for a moment about some of the words and phrases you might use in describing management: controlling behavior; reaching students; assigning detention; being tardy; covering content; being ahead or behind in teaching content. These traditional metaphors reveal something about power relationships among teachers, students, administrators, and parents. They sound a great deal like words that were used to describe American factory work at the turn of the 20th century (McLaughlin, 1994).

Two overarching themes of the factory model of schooling are obedience and control. As McLaughlin (1994) suggested, "a major purpose of authority—and the uses of power—in the obedience perspective is to maintain adult control over younger people" (p. 76). This is akin to high-level managers in a factory maintaining control over low-level workers who are expected to comply with existing norms and be obedient to these norms regardless of personal needs.

These traditional terms matter because they may guide your thinking about classroom practice. Unless you consciously explore your metaphorical ways of thinking, you may be unable to understand how you presently view student discipline and whether alternative approaches to management and discipline may improve your classroom practice. You might remain inhibited for many years by the metaphorical perspectives handed down as truisms of practice from one generation of teachers to the next at a time when contemporary society has called into question traditional metaphors for management.

We offer one alternative metaphor—*negotiation*—as a way of thinking about management and discipline. It is intended to pique your curiosity about your relationships with students and offer you a pathway for thinking more carefully about how traditional factorylike metaphors may be less relevant in today's classrooms.

Rather than regarding yourself as the sole source of authority in the classroom, think about the classroom as a place where teachers share power. To assume this stance, you must be willing to give up the idea of having total control over students, and instead view students as having a voice in classroom decision making. Sharing power does not mean relinquishing all responsibility for deciding what goes on in your classroom; it means bringing students into your classroom decision-making process more often.

The idea of negotiation is not new, yet when it is applied to schools it has powerful implications for management and student discipline. This raises an important question: What exactly do you negotiate with students? The answer is both simple and complex. You negotiate almost everything, including rules, curriculum, assessment strategies, and classroom social interactions. Again, we are not advocating taking power away from the teacher and investing it in students. The metaphor of negotiation suggests that students are given greater voice in making decisions about curriculum and instruction and how they would like to approach their own learning.

**CCSSO Principle 6: Communication**

Alfie Kohn (2006), who writes and lectures extensively on education and human behavior, is an ardent advocate of sharing power with students. Kohn cites the following beneficial effects of sharing power with students:

- Students have the opportunity to practice participatory skills necessary for participation in a democracy.
- Academic achievement improves when students have choice.
- Teachers who share power with students find their work more interesting.
- Relieved of the onus of constantly monitoring and controlling behavior, teachers are free to interact with students on issues that really matter.

Many questions about management and discipline can be posed to students: What kind of environment do we want this classroom to be? How should we decorate our classroom walls? How should the furniture be arranged? What should people do when they finish a project early? How much noise is too much?

When you think of a classroom as a community whose members have a stake in what goes on there, you can more easily imagine providing structured opportunities–regular and impromptu class meetings–for members to meet and make decisions. The decision-making process consists of talking, listening, and generating possible solutions to problems. Kohn argues that reaching consensus on general goals and guidelines is preferable to voting on specific rules and procedures, because in the process of decision making students learn and practice the skills of participatory democracy.

Sharing power does not mean abdicating power. You are still the responsible adult while giving guidance, asking questions, and offering suggestions rather than laying down laws. Ways to share power include taking turns at making decisions (e.g., you choose what to read on Friday afternoon 1 week; the students choose the next); limiting options available to ensure that students choose materials and activities that are appropriate and have educational value (e.g., sleeping on Friday afternoons is not an option); and setting parameters by specifying goals but letting students decide how to get there (e.g., how can we keep the noise level down when you are working in groups?). Teacher-student negotiation is part of sharing power, and you are a member of the community as well.

The barriers to implementing an alternative management metaphor of shared power are formidable. You may work in a state, district, or school that makes negotiating some aspects of teaching and learning difficult. For example, rarely are students or teachers able to negotiate on the issue of standardized tests. Furthermore, many teachers are resistant to the idea of sharing power. After all, autocracy is a less time-consuming, simpler form of government than democracy. Many teachers are so steeped in the traditional metaphor of control that the only alternative they can imagine is chaos. Most discouragingly, students themselves may resist sharing power. Like teachers, they may have become so accustomed to traditional power roles that they may refuse to make decisions or simply parrot what they've learned from prior experience (e.g., "People who come in late should have to stay after school for 15 minutes."). Students may also test a teacher's commitment to sharing power by proposing outrageous solutions (e.g., "Everyone gets A's, no matter what.").

Despite these barriers, we encourage you to consider negotiating some aspects of your classroom. If we are sincere when we say we want students to be problem-solvers, decision-makers, and risk-takers, then we must seriously question the assumptions about power and control in traditional approaches to management and discipline (Boomer, Lester, Onore, & Cook, 1992; Joseph & Efron, 2005).

## SUMMARY

We began this chapter by describing how Joseph began teaching believing that managing a classroom and discipline were synonymous. Thanks to his mentor teacher, he learned that classroom management encompasses managing information, time, student behavior, student records, student learning, and student work. This chapter has emphasized the human dimension of classroom management and discipline.

- Knowing who your students are will help you to become an effective and a successful classroom manager, as will knowing who you are as a manager, disciplinarian, and negotiator.
- Academic theories of discipline provide specific guidance for dealing with discipline problems, but are difficult to implement in their entirety. Most often, teachers use them eclectically.
- Classroom management consists of practical, cultural, and metaphorical elements.
- The metaphor of classroom management as negotiation may be more appropriate for 21st-century classrooms than the metaphor of classroom as factory.

Classroom management and student discipline are probably two of your greatest concerns as you think about teaching. This is both normal and understandable. Yet you will eventually discover that the vast majority of management and discipline challenges are minor and easily solved.

### *Reflecting on the Standards*

- What are your beliefs about the kind of classroom manager and disciplinarian you will be? How will you go about establishing a positive learning climate in your classroom and in your school?
- To what extent are you committed to establishing democratic values and processes in your classroom?
- How and when do you see yourself negotiating and sharing power?

# CHAPTER 4

# Considering Curriculum for Middle and High School Students

Designing and implementing a classroom curriculum that engages all students is fundamental to effective teaching and learning. If you begin your teaching career without knowing how students' backgrounds align or misalign with classroom curriculum and instruction, then you may, albeit unknowingly, distance some students from what you teach and from the learning environment you create. The goal of this chapter is to help you broaden your perspective of curriculum by understanding its multiple dimensions. This chapter is primarily related to CCSSO Principle #7: *The teacher plans instruction based upon the knowledge of the subject matter, students, the community, and curriculum goals.*

This chapter focuses on factors that come into play as teachers make decisions about what is appropriate for a particular group of students to learn. Specifically, this chapter will help you:

- Define and evaluate curriculum;
- Consider how national, state, district, and school standards have influenced curriculum;
- Examine the relationship between textbooks and other instructional materials in helping teachers bridge the gap between curriculum goals and students' experiences, needs, interests, and aptitudes;
- Identify the role culture plays in classroom curriculum;
- Become familiar with developmentally appropriate curriculum.

In today's classrooms, you must have a firm grasp of the content you are teaching. But you must also know your students and help them to connect socially, personally, and culturally with what you teach and how you teach. From this perspective, your classroom curriculum reflects the interface between students' personal qualities and the content to be learned. This is significantly different from the perspective of curriculum that Joseph accepted as he began his career and during his first 8 years of teaching.

## *REFLECTING ON PRACTICE:*
## JOSEPH BRAUN–"CLUELESS ABOUT CURRICULUM"

I began my teaching career as the middle school social studies teacher in a parochial school very much like the one I had attended only 10 years before. At this point in my professional development I had taken no education courses, so curriculum was just a long, tricky word to spell. I was almost clueless as to what it meant: It was "the stuff" the kids were supposed to learn–in other words, the content in the textbook.

Before the school year began, the principal handed me the textbook and said she expected me to cover all of the chapters before the end of the school year. This was my first lesson learned about curriculum: A school administrator has the function of communicating to teachers *what* content is to be taught as well as *how* it will be taught.

In all fairness to the principal, she did support me as I struggled to manage my classroom and provide solid curriculum to the students. She did this by showing me the integral relationship between the objective of the lesson and the assessment–these should mirror each other, she explained to me. This was curriculum lesson number two: Assessment is integral to knowing whether students are learning anything.

That first year I didn't finish all the books assigned to me in September. I explained to the principal that when my students were particularly inquisitive about certain information, or when they seemed puzzled by concepts, I decided to spend more time on these sections than originally intended. Understandingly, she commended my flexibility. She wished me well as I moved into my second year of teaching and a new, public school. The lesson learned: A good administrator recognizes teachers must make professionally responsible decisions about curriculum.

As a middle school social studies teacher, I provided students with a certain kind of classroom curriculum. Had I been more aware of the many factors that influence curriculum, I might have made better connections between my students and the curriculum. Teaching content is important, but considering the interests and needs of the students being taught is more important than the amount of information covered. Over the years I have realized that curriculum means more than covering a textbook and filling students' heads with facts. I have spent most of my career in higher education providing preservice teachers with alternatives to that interpretation of curriculum.

### *Questions to Consider*

- What experiences in your life are relevant to creating curriculum for middle and high school students?

- How did the curriculum change as you progressed through school?
- How were the values of the community in which you grew up reflected in the school curriculum you experienced?
- Can you recall any instances of controversy over the curriculum?

## CASE STUDY:
## A TALE OF TEACHING BIOLOGY IN TWO CITIES

Professor Rick Mead's (a pseudonym) first job as a teacher educator was at a university offering off-campus, field-based programs and internships to students working on their master's degrees after completing student teaching. Rick was assigned to supervise interns in several small, rural communities, some located as far as 80 miles from the university. One of them was Plainsville (a pseudonym). Plainsville's economy and the ethos of its schools were centered on wheat farming and cattle ranching. A community of approximately one thousand predominately Protestant, White individuals and composed of middle- and working-class families, Plainsville was proud of its schools. In politically conservative and strongly religious Plainsville, Rick learned the following: what teachers do not teach and could not teach were as much a part of the curriculum as what was taught. Plainsville taught him that the *null curriculum*–the subject matter content that educators purposely do not teach in school–affects students as much as content that is taught.

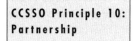

CCSSO Principle 10: Partnership

Rick Mead came face to face with the null curriculum in his first meeting with the district curriculum administrator. He was supervising an intern teaching biology, and as the administrator familiarized him with the district philosophy and curriculum materials, it was made very clear that in Plainsville the intern would not be allowed to teach evolution and natural selection. In fact, the administrator identified the exact textbook pages to be avoided. Later in the semester, the intern wanted to show a video in biology class tracing human development during gestation and depicting a few seconds of birth at the end. Rick suggested he check with the principal about this portion of the video. The principal expressed surprise that the intern would even consider showing such footage and instructed the intern to turn off the VCR during the last 8 seconds of the video, if he wanted to show it at all.

Clearly, in Plainsville, individuals rather than textbook publishers were making decisions about content. The decision-making process, embodied in community values and overseen by school administrators, was also central to the school's curriculum.

Meanwhile, Rick was also supervising another biology intern in Edgetown (a pseudonym) with a population of about 20,000. Edgetown was also predominately White, rural, middle-class, and Protestant. Edgetown, however, was the home of Rick's university. Some of the more progressive ideas from the university influenced the community and Edgetown High School.

Here, the intern freely taught about evolution and natural selection and without anyone questioning whether he should show videos depicting biological events. Only 80 miles from Plainsville, this intern had freedom as a professional to make decisions about the information most appropriate for helping Edgetown students learn science content. Preparing students for college was highly valued, and the administrators expected a college-preparatory science curriculum.

What can we learn about who influences curriculum from this tale of biology in two cities? There are many influences on the curriculum. Undeniably, textbook publishers have long-standing, major influence in deciding what is included in any curriculum. School administrators, representing the communities where they work, influence curriculum, both null and otherwise. The interns, too, had an influence on what was taught as they made content decisions. Thus, not only do community values influence the school's curriculum, but a teacher's values influence and become part of the school curriculum.

Although the events in this case study happened over 30 years ago, debates about teaching the origins of life continue. Current controversies involve the teaching of "intelligent design" (the idea that a "master architect" directed the development of life) versus evolution. For example, a number of parents in a south-central Pennsylvania school district recently sued, halting a policy requiring all ninth-grade students to learn about intelligent design alongside evolution (Cavanagh, 2005). Biology isn't the only contentious subject. What controversies about curriculum exist in your subject area?

## TOWARD A DEFINITION OF CURRICULUM

As you begin to formulate a personally meaningful and valid definition of curriculum, you will become aware that it is shaped by myriad factors, that it gives shape to students' lives in and out of school, and that it may be more culturally relevant and engaging for some students than others. When you relate questions about curriculum to specific communities, minority groups, socioeconomic groups, and gender issues (among other sociocultural factors), you can see how challenging it becomes to define curriculum. Consider the definition below (Cuban, 1996):

A curriculum of a classroom, school, district, state (or nation) is a series of planned events intended for students to learn particular knowledge, skills, and values and organized to be carried out by administrators and teachers. This concept of curriculum stresses purposes, content, organization, relationships, and outcomes for students. (p. 221)

As you consider this definition, address the following questions alone or with peers.

- What parts of the definition, if any, align with the curricula of the elementary, middle, and high schools you attended?
- In what ways is the definition culturally sensitive?

Consider minor or major revisions to Cuban's definition. Make the necessary changes to arrive at a new definition of curriculum. Explain the changes you or your group made and share your new definition.

## WHO DECIDES? CURRICULUM AT THE NATIONAL, STATE, DISTRICT, SCHOOL, AND CLASSROOM LEVELS

Decisions about what content to teach and how to teach it are made on multiple levels, including national, state, district, school, and classroom (Armstrong, 2002). Teachers do not always agree with the curriculum decisions made for them, and some ignore these decisions or simply refuse to comply with them. For example, when the intern Rick Mead was supervising began teaching in Plainsville, decisions about excluding specific content from the classroom science curriculum had already been made at the district level. As a new teacher in the district, the intern received these decisions and was expected to comply. He could make decisions about how to teach selected content, but not about what content to teach. Not only did he inherit policymakers' decisions, but he also inherited community values that were embedded in these decisions, and that were embedded historically in the school's tradition of teaching and learning.

**CCSSO Principle 10: Community**

### National Efforts to Influence Curriculum

The framers of the U.S. Constitution did not directly address education, preferring to leave it up to the states. Thus, the federal government did not become directly involved in education until the Soviet Union launched Sputnik in 1958 during the Cold War. Because leaders believed that an educated youth was critical to our nation's success in the race for space, in 1965 the Elementary and Secondary Education Act (ESEA) became one of the first sources of large amounts of federal funding for the development of school curriculum.

The next major federal push to influence curriculum and learning occurred in 1983 with the publication of *A Nation at Risk*, a report by the Department of Education that had a major impact on education (available at http://www.ed.gov/pubs/NatAtRisk/index.html). This report found "disturbing inadequacies" in the way education was designed and conducted in the nation's schools. The authors referred to the curriculum as a "smorgasbord" and called for more challenging and uniform content, higher expectations for students, more time spent on academics both in and out of school, and stronger leadership and fiscal support for schools. These recommendations led to the first National Education Summit, held in 1989, where governors made commitments to persuade their respective state departments of education to create a more rigorous curriculum for all students. This together with the 1994 passage of the *Goals 2000: Educate America Act* sparked the standards movement.

Leadership in the standards movement was initially provided by professional educational organizations. *Curriculum and Evaluation Standards for School Mathematics*, published by the National Council for Teachers of Mathematics (1989), was the first

> **CCSSO Principle 10:**
> **Community**

of many standards documents published by professional organizations representing the subject areas of the curriculum. These professional organization standards became the blueprints used by state departments of education as they individually adopted state-level standards.

In some states, such as Illinois, this was the first time the state had provided guidelines to local districts delineating precisely what students should know and be able to do upon reaching a certain grade level and, ultimately, graduation. Other states, such as California, had been providing such guidelines to local districts long before *A Nation at Risk* was published and the standards movement launched. All states, with the exception of Iowa, had developed their own individual discipline-based learning standards and benchmarks by the time George W. Bush became president and formulated a landmark piece of legislation known as No Child Left Behind (NCLB).

The No Child Left Behind (NCLB) Act was signed into law on January 8, 2002, as part of the renewal of ESEA, which earmarks education money for the states. Features of NCLB that are particularly relevant for prospective middle and high school teachers include: 1. Increased accountability—every state is required to implement statewide accountability systems covering all public schools and students; 2. More choices for students and parents—students attending schools that fail to demonstrate adequate progress must be given the opportunity to attend a better public school; 3. Highly qualified teachers–all teachers in core academic areas must be highly qualified in the core academic subjects they teach.

The national standards movement has been praised for leveling the playing field by informing all stakeholders of, for example, what is meant by the term *science*, why science is taught in middle and high schools, what science knowledge is most important, and how best to teach science. Many critics, however, argue that the movement is leading the country closer to a national curriculum, which they believe is counter to the fundamental nature of schooling in the United States. According to critics, a national curriculum would deprive parents, students, and teachers of their important roles in influencing the development and implementation of local curricula (Noddings, 1997; Reigeluth, 1997). Theodore Sizer (2003) described the standards and accountability movement as well intentioned but undermined by the context of poverty in which 20% of our youth grow up. In his view, a focus on standards and testing draws much-needed attention and resources away from the root problem of poverty, which is detrimental to the academic performance of so many students.

There are other criticisms. Some disciplines, such as social studies and the fine arts, have been left out of the picture of reform painted by NCLB. One result is that these subjects are being marginalized in the curriculum. Arts programs have been drastically reduced or cut from the curriculum in many of the nation's roughly 15,000 school districts. State departments of education, which are charged with tracking all the data generated by testing and other elements of NCLB, don't have the capacity to assume the entire monitoring burden placed on them by NCLB (Lewis, 2005).

Despite its numerous critics and shortcomings, a revision of the original NCLB legislation was recently reauthorized and some of the above-mentioned problems are being addressed. In short, the federal government has assumed a growing role in the development of school curriculum and that trend is not likely to go away.

## State Curriculum Initiatives: High-Stakes Testing

While national professional organizations and their participants hold no legal authority for mandating curriculum, state boards and departments of education, or similar agencies, do. Thus, rather than developing national tests for measuring Adequate Yearly Progress (AYP), NCLB requires state departments of education to carry out the testing. Since NCLB was based on President Bush's experience in reforming education while governor of Texas, that state provides a representative example of the impact of high-stakes testing.

CCSSO Principle 8: Assessment

The Texas Assessment of Knowledge and Skills (TAKS) is a state-mandated standardized high-stakes test, as NCLB intended. Significant consequences are attached to student performance on the test. Low-performing schools can be put on academic probation. On the other hand, when students at a particular school do exceptionally well, teachers might receive pay bonuses, and students might be rewarded with special treats. Not surprisingly, the test has an important influence on school curriculum and instruction. Because of pressure for high scores on the TAKS, many Texas teachers have begun teaching to the test. That is, in some classrooms, the curriculum consists of what is likely to be on the test and not much more.

Although the TAKS may frustrate some Texas teachers who would prefer more curricular autonomy, the test is nevertheless a reality. Teachers who value their jobs and who have students' best interests in the forefront of their instruction believe they must prepare students for the test. This means that their classroom curriculum must, at least in part, reflect the content and skills required to do well on the TAKS. As a result of the standards movement and NCLB, the trend has been for curriculum to be more closely and carefully defined at the state level. Much decision making about curriculum has been removed from local curriculum leaders and classroom teachers.

## District, School, and Classroom Curriculum Initiatives

Curriculum decision making and development at the district level are often the responsibility of curriculum leaders, who are usually former teachers recognized for their expertise and knowledge. As a rule, the size of the district determines the number and type of curriculum leaders. Large school districts might have an assistant superintendent for curriculum who oversees the activities of curriculum leaders in each subject area and for various grade levels. Small school districts, however, might have only one person who has responsibility for curriculum activities of the whole district. District-level curriculum leaders have the responsibility of helping classroom teachers, key players in local curriculum development activities, align their intended content with state regulations.

Although every level of curriculum development is important, the two most significant levels are the school and classroom. The school and the classroom are where curriculum is actually implemented, where curriculum is transformed into daily lessons, and where teachers and students interface to create unique contexts for learning. The school, as a curriculum context, has the responsibility of linking state and district curriculum guidelines with classroom instruction. In an era of high-stakes testing, this linkage is often of paramount importance.

Classroom-level curriculum work is very practical, and teacher wisdom is central to knowing how best to meet state and district requirements while providing students with meaningful, relevant, and useful lessons.

## MODELS OF CURRICULUM DEVELOPMENT

One of this country's most influential theorists of curriculum was Ralph Tyler (1902–1994). He posed four major questions that still serve to guide curriculum construction at the school and classroom level: 1. What are the purposes of the school? 2. What educational experiences are likely to help attain these purposes? 3. How should these experiences be organized? 4. How should learning be assessed? (Tyler, 1979). More currently, Wiggins and McTighe (2005) have averred that the last of these questions should be first. That is, assessment is the most crucial element of the curriculum and once the topic and essential questions of a unit are determined, the assessment should be the first of the four tasks accomplished. With this end in view, the rest of the curriculum can be planned backwards.

One way to evaluate whether a curriculum is truly highly engaging, as well as aligned to state content standards, is to view it through a set of curriculum design standards. Table 4.1 represents a set of standards published by the National Council for the Social Studies. These questions can be used to evaluate curriculum units in a variety of subjects. As you gain experience, you may want to seek out evaluation tools specific to your subject areas.

## DECIDING WHO REALLY MAKES THE CURRICULUM

Many stakeholders and various factors are at work—and often in tension—as school curricula are developed and implemented. Three additional factors, however, profoundly influence the nature of the classroom curriculum: textbooks, individual and shared characteristics of students and their communities, and developmental or age-level characteristics of students. Each of these factors is discussed below.

### Understanding the Role of
### Textbooks in Your Classroom Curriculum

While textbooks have been the mainstay for middle and high school instruction, they have not been without criticism. For example, textbooks have been charged with narrowing the focus of instruction, determining the curriculum of schools and classrooms, and disempowering classroom

## TABLE 4.1. Standards for Evaluating Units of Study

| | |
|---|---|
| **Reflective Thinking** | Does the unit pose problems that challenge students to figure out possible answers, solutions, or results by thinking for themselves? |
| | Do the focus questions and intended learning outcomes (benchmarks) that guide a unit of study challenge students to produce their own meaning rather than to retrieve information? |
| | Are students invited to solve problems or make decisions by reflecting upon what they already know and upon accumulated knowledge that is new to them? |
| | Do the problems or issues posed by the curriculum prompt students to consider more than one response rather than merely to recite a scripted correct answer? |
| **Coherence** | To what extent are the separate parts of the curriculum plan, i.e., focus questions, benchmarks, key concepts, instructional resources, and lessons interrelated? |
| | Is the unit of study a coherent inquiry about a focused topic rather than a fragmentary and disembodied set of activities? |
| **Depth** | Is the number of focus questions and benchmarks limited so that the unit encourages depth of knowledge? |
| | Is meaningful understanding of each key concept thoughtfully developed by the lessons of the unit? |
| **Alignment** | Is the curriculum unit aligned with valid external curriculum content standards? |
| | Are statements of what students are expected to learn aligned with assessment tasks they perform to provide evidence of their learning? |
| | Are all benchmarks for the unit assessed? |
| | Does each assessment task enable the teacher to gauge the degree to which a student has reached one of the benchmarks? |
| **Knowledge Application** | Is the curriculum designed to engage students in addressing real problems or issues they are likely to encounter beyond school? |
| | Is the answer to "Why do we have to learn this?" evident in the curriculum plan, which embodies a real problem or issue that people actually face in life? |

Adapted from Harris & Yocum, 2000, p. 32.

teachers (Apple, 1993). Many people believe that textbooks publishers govern what is taught in school. Tanner and Tanner (2006) argue, however, that such exclusive governance of school content is a myth because publishers are concerned with meeting market demands that take into account the informational needs of teachers and students based on state standards.

Textbook companies respond to controversial topics such as evolution and creationism in a manner that will be acceptable to as many educators and citizens as possible without lowering sales and profits. Science isn't the only subject that deals with controversial content. For example, publishers and writers of social studies textbooks continuously struggle with how to appropriately and satisfactorily depict historical events and societal groups within the American experience. Try to think of examples of controversial content in textbooks in areas such as English, health, family living, and physical education. Ultimately, when companies try to make their books all things to all people, the result can be bland textbook content that eliminates treatment of important, but sometimes volatile, social issues.

Textbooks continue to be used extensively. When used wisely and effectively, they can help teachers and students alike. In today's classrooms, however, where both teachers and students can utilize new technologies to access information easily and instantaneously, there is a growing awareness that textbooks provide only one source of classroom content.

## Culturally Relevant Curriculum

Another essential facet of school curriculum is its cultural dimension. Over the past two decades, this dimension has received considerable attention from a variety of educators, particularly those

> **CCSSO Principle 3:**
> **Adapting Instruction**

concerned with providing every student opportunities to be successful in school (see Gay, 2000; Ladson-Billings, 1994).

Culturally relevant teaching assumes that meaningful teaching is sensitive to cultural phenomena and to forces in communities surrounding the school and in students' lives as they are shaped by these communities. Culturally relevant curricula focus on four important questions:

- How are students engaged with the content?
- How are students invited to learn by teachers?
- How are students invited and encouraged to interact with one another in the midst of school-related activities and events?
- How do teachers respond to students' personal backgrounds and to students' communities where these backgrounds are shaped?

### Developmentally Appropriate Curriculum

Curriculum must also be developmentally appropriate for students' cognitive, physical, social, and emotional needs. Most educators would agree that a 12-year-old has different developmental needs from a 16-year-old high school junior, and from a 19-year-old high

| CCSSO Principle 2: |
| Learning and |
| Human Development |

school senior with Down Syndrome. All three students share the same basic needs—food, shelter, clothing, and a caring home environment. Yet all have differing needs. For example, the high school junior might be preparing to attend college or vocational school, while the middle schooler may not be thinking of these things yet. The high school senior's transition into the world of work is imminent. Because of their differing developmental needs, the three students' educational needs differ as well. The first may still be wondering whether she should become an astronaut or an actress. The second might be concerned about SAT scores or about completing a special high school program assuring her entry into a related program at a community college. The third might be concerned about performing well in her community-based placement at a supermarket.

***Middle School Curriculum.*** For decades, educators adhered to the belief that early adolescents had the same kind of learning needs as older adolescents. Consequently, a similar kind of content-centered curriculum was implemented for both groups. For 10- to 14-year-olds, this curriculum arrangement was called the junior high school and, as the name implies, was designed as a preparation for high school. Traditional junior high schools are organized into subject departments and often place students in academic tracks. Students move from class to class and from teacher to teacher every 50 minutes or so.

More recently, however, increased attention has been given to the developmental characteristics and needs of early adolescents. A landmark paper commissioned by the Carnegie Corporation concluded that the high school curriculum model was not well suited to early adolescents, and an alternative curriculum and school structure were needed to better meet the developmental needs of these students (Carnegie Council on Adolescent Development, 1989). The resulting middle school movement has caused educators everywhere to rethink the nature of schooling for 10- to 14-year-olds (Stevenson, 2002). Middle schools attempt to reach two goals: to make curriculum more responsive to the needs of early adolescents, and to help ease the transition from self-contained elementary classroom environments to multiperiod secondary classroom environments.

***High School Curriculum.*** The high school curriculum model has remained relatively stable for years. Tour most high schools in the nation and you will find a similar curriculum structure and schooling experience. Most high school days are segmented into six or seven 50-minute periods, although some high schools offer block scheduling, which extends the instructional period to approximately 90 minutes. Whatever the time allotment for instruction, bells or tones signify the beginning and end of these segments. School buildings are usually divided into areas, wings, or corridors where certain classes are taught: For example, all science classes are taught in the science corridor. Such arrangements make it easier for science teachers to interact and share materials but make it more difficult for teachers of different subjects to coordinate or collaborate on instruction.

Another enduring feature of high schools is tracking: grouping students according to perceived academic ability. Students in many high schools are still put into some form of academically homogeneous

| CCSSO Principle 3: Adapting Instruction |

track, even though tracking is of dubious benefit to students, particularly those placed in lower tracks (Oakes, 1985). Many high schools have extensive vocational programs and shop classes, while schools located outside metropolitan areas might offer agricultural education classes. High school students tend to be known individually by their academic track, or by the nature of their selected educational program (e.g., college-bound, vocational, business education). To graduate from high school, students are generally required to have successfully earned a certain number of credits, called Carnegie Units. While credits vary slightly from one state to another, most high school students must complete credits in mathematics, English, history, science, and physical education.

Many high schools offer Advanced Placement (AP) courses preparing college-bound students to take the AP Tests administered by the Educational Testing Service (ETS). ETS provides course syllabi to guide high school teachers in preparing students for AP Tests. Advanced Placement courses are both prestigious and popular with high-achieving students, because college credit is given for scoring well on an AP Test. One high school reform strategy that has gained popularity is extending to all students the opportunity, formerly limited to an elite few, to take Advanced Placement courses and tests.

## SUMMARY

As you reflect on the contents of this chapter and anticipate teaching in a specific school and community, begin thinking about which issues might influence your classroom curriculum. Think also about how your own perspectives, beliefs, and values will influence your classroom curriculum and the curriculum of the school where you might teach.

Because curriculum is complex and multidimensional, you will likely broaden and deepen your understanding of it over time. As you gain a better understanding of how personal, social, political, religious, academic, and cultural factors influence the curriculum you teach and the materials you use, you will be better prepared to meet the educational needs of your students. Among the key points to remember are:

- The development of national and state standards dominated curriculum initiatives in the 1980s and 1990s, just as NCLB has dominated the early years of the 21st century.
- At the state level, high-stakes testing and accountability increasingly influence the classroom curriculum.
- Much curriculum development occurs at the district and school levels. Teachers have the ultimate responsibility for transforming the intended curriculum into daily instructional activities and interactions with students.
- Textbooks can be useful tools for organizing and implementing classroom curriculum, but like all tools they have strengths and limitations.
- Culturally relevant curriculum is student-centered; ensures that students' needs are addressed before, during, and after the presentation of the intended curriculum; and offers students multiple pathways to learning skills, knowledge, and attitudes.
- Curriculum should be developmentally appropriate. Some middle schools and high schools are restructuring the curriculum to meet students' developmental needs.

### Reflecting on the Standards

- Where do you stand on the content-centered/student-centered continuum of curriculum?
- What sources will you draw upon to create curriculum in your classroom?
- How important is content in your subject area? What is the role of the textbook in your subject area?
- How can you make the curriculum in your subject area culturally relevant?
- How would curriculum in your classroom differ from middle to high school level?
- What value do you see in national and state curriculum initiatives?

# CHAPTER 5

# Planning for Middle and High School Instruction

Why plan for instruction? Planning allows teachers to organize what they wish to do for the year or semester, in a unit of instruction or in a particular lesson. Second, it leads to meaningful instruction that facilitates student learning. Third, planning allows for the articulation of subject matter, what we termed in the previous chapter "the intended curriculum." The art curriculum in a high school, for example, is planned as Art I, Art II, Art III, and so on. Fourth, good planning provides teachers with the opportunity to address individual needs. Fifth, it minimizes management and discipline problems; students are less apt to involve themselves in off-task behavior when they know what is expected of them.

The purpose of this chapter is primarily related to CCSSO Principle #7: *The teacher plans instruction based upon knowledge of subject matter, students, the community, and curriculum goals.*

Specifically, this chapter will help you:

- Identify why teachers plan for instruction;
- Describe how they use contextual information;
- Understand short-range and long-term planning;
- Survey two approaches to standards-based planning;
- Plan a unit and lesson in your subject area.

Effective teachers know how to plan instruction that creates a bridge between students' life experiences and the goals of the curriculum. They know how to use students' responses to instruction to adjust their plans.

### REFLECTING ON PRACTICE: JESUS GARCIA– "TEACHING A PERSONAL INTERPRETATION OF HISTORY"

I grew up in a community where most minorities lived "on the other side of the tracks." The public schools I attended, however, were integrated. While most students graduated from high school, only a few minorities enrolled in the prestigious universities located in the San Francisco Bay Area; some joined the armed forces; most assumed entry-level positions at the local factories that dotted the area. I left my community knowing about the practice of tracking and societal forces–racism and discrimination.

I began teaching in the 1960s by appointing myself the expert in United States history. I had earned a baccalaureate degree, majoring in history with a specialization in the experiences of minorities (African, Mexican, Asian, and Native Americans). I had grown up at a time when Americans were raising questions about the nation's domestic and foreign policies. I had learned from the popular press about America's treatment of its citizens and its policies toward Latin America and other parts of the world.

I taught at the high school level and was responsible for courses in U.S. history. My students were culturally diverse and each year entered my classroom with a variety of strengths and challenges. Regardless of their needs, I was determined to integrate the historical experiences of Mexican Americans into my U.S. history classes. When I found the textbook wanting, I reviewed other materials describing this group's experiences and included essential information into my instructional program. I was not going to lose the opportunity to highlight the exploitation of Mexican Americans at the hands of Anglo Americans!

As I planned for instruction, it never occurred to me to reflect on whether my students needed my personal interpretation of U.S. history or how my interpretation of U.S. history fit into effective social studies education as described by leading educators of the time. In my planning I had not given much thought to the purpose of schools, a definition of social studies, or the purpose of social studies in my school district. My students learned U.S. history according to Jesus Garcia.

### Questions for Reflection

- As you reflect on your K–12 and college experiences, what teachers come to mind as either highly effective or ineffective planners?
- What lasting impressions do you have of teachers who promoted their particular interpretations of a school subject?

## WHAT DO TEACHERS BRING TO THE PLANNING TABLE?

Teachers employ an array of information when planning. As a result of their teacher education experiences, they are familiar with documents describing the purposes of education, subject area standards documents, and specific planning approaches. In this section we describe some of what teachers bring to the planning table.

## Identifying Purposes of Education

What should be the purpose(s) of education? Many of the goals (e.g., command of fundamental processes, health, citizenship, vocational preparation) noted in *The Cardinal Principles of Secondary Education*, a report compiled by the National Education Association's Commission on the Reorganization of Secondary Education (1918), can be found in contemporary documents. This suggests that the purpose of schools has not changed significantly over time but our expectations of schools have. Three of the goals listed in Goals 2000 state that K–12 schools will maintain a 90% graduation rate; students will be first in the world in mathematics and science achievement; and adult Americans will be literate, possess the skills to complete in a global society, and know and practice the dispositions of active citizens.

Today, many educators, politicians, and parents are calling for a greater focus on the aims and purpose of schools (Ravitch & Finn, 1989). The command of fundamental processes (e.g., reading, writing, mathematics), for example, remains a high priority and has expanded to mean mastering the uses of technology.

## Conceptualizing Subject Areas

Have you thought about the purpose of teaching your subject area? For example, some teachers have conceptualized the purpose of social studies as promoting citizenship. They subscribe to one or more of the following approaches to achieving this purpose: 1. the transmission of the nation's history, traditions, and values; 2. an exploration and study of one or more of the social science disciplines; 3. an examination of contemporary issues and problems; and 4. providing for the well-being of the individual (Allen & Stevens, 1997).

> CCSSO Principle 1:
> Knowledge of the Subject
> and
> CCSSO Principle 3:
> Adapting for Instruction

Teachers adopt a particular conceptualization of a subject area based on a number of factors, including their personal experiences, preparation, and classroom experiences. Today, standards documents exist for most major subject areas in the K–12 curriculum. These documents help teachers align their personal definitions of a subject area and its purpose(s) with the views of leading educators.

## APPROACHES TO STANDARDS-BASED PLANNING

Articulation of subject matter and addressing student needs are two reasons teachers plan for instruction. Teachers who begin with subject matter are described as *subject-based.* These teachers first identify the essential knowledge, skills, and dispositions associated with a discipline or topic under study. They may review essential documents as they look to textbooks and other material to guide their planning. Once the initial planning begins, they also reflect on student needs.

A second group—those who focus on student needs—are described as *student-based.* While these teachers are aware of the essential knowledge of their subject area, they allow the informal and formal assessing they do in the classroom to guide planning. They pay particular attention to student interests, academic strengths and weaknesses, and societal challenges and issues when developing instruction. However, they too turn to essential documents to align their planning.

A third approach is *outcomes-based* because teachers turn to the standards in their discipline areas to initiate planning while asking: "What should students know and be able to do upon completion of this unit?" and "How will students show what they know and can do?" Teachers who use this form of planning consider content, activities, and students' needs, but they use a different process, which is referred to as *backwards planning.* Backwards planning begins with the end in view and then builds the paths that students can take to reach that end (Wiggins & McTighe, 2005).

Effective teachers usually take an eclectic approach to planning; they know that a single approach to planning will not be adequate in today's classrooms. Experience has made them sensitive to sequence; the unpredictable relations between teacher, students, and subject area; the porous boundaries among them; and how decision making continuously shifts as the day-to-day happenings of school life influence what occurs in the classroom.

### Theory into Practice: Considering Student Needs in Planning

Toni Wolfe (a pseudonym) teaches in an urban alternative high school. As you read her reflection on her students' characteristics, think about how these may influence her planning.

> I've come to realize that what most kids really need is simply to know that someone cares for them. Perhaps this caring comes in the form of a compliment, verbal encouragement, or even a smile and a hello (which some kids will never see during the day if not from us). Or, if you're a daring teacher, you know that sometimes kids really

do just need a hug. Recently, I had one of those teaching days that reinforces this in my mind.

First, there is Karen [a pseudonym] who had her 2-year-old taken away from her 3 weeks ago because the baby's father wants to be in his life (after 2-and-a-half years of absence) and is trying to prove she is an unfit parent. Unfit parent? Karen. Who gets up at 3:30 a.m. every morning to walk an hour to the bus stop and change buses five times just to get to school on time, who pulled straight A's last quarter, and who works until 11:00 p.m. five nights a week to support herself and her son. She can't see her son until the next court date–January 10. Today is November 25. Imagine her Christmas knowing the man stopping her from seeing her child is not only bringing false charges against her but also just impregnated a 14-year-old who won't press charges against him. Do I sit there and let her cry in front of me? Does my professionalism limit me from showing any emotion?

What about Mario [a pseudonym], who is constantly sleeping in class but who woke up long enough to write his personal narrative? He brought it to my desk and read it aloud to me. It was a story about how when he was 13 he and his older brother went to a friend's house. His brother's friend, Ernie, had grabbed a magnum and said, "I wonder what the world would be like without Ernie?" pulled the trigger, and killed himself in front of my now 17-year-old student. Tears began to roll down his face as he tried to choke them back and continue reading. Oh yeah, he works until 11:00 every night just so he can send money to help with the baby he hasn't seen in 9 months. The mother, who used to be his best friend, won't answer his calls or tell him where they live.

Life happens in the classroom because the classroom is a microcosm of our communities. The classroom is as much the "real world" as the world the students enter after the final bell rings, and they will always need support and encouragement. Education is more than learning how to read, write, and do arithmetic. Students are individuals with minds and emotions. How can I educate someone to be a good, caring citizen without caring myself and modeling what that is? Not all my students will remember to put a comma after an introductory clause, but I sincerely hope they learn that they've gained their biggest fan who will forever offer her encouragement, enthusiasm, and support.

***Questions to Consider.*** Teaching in an alternative school is no easy task. Teachers who work in these settings are often extraordinary individuals who give their all to help students. Young adults who enroll in these schools often come with troubled pasts and may be using their "last chance" to salvage their educational careers. The experiences of Karen and Mario, however, are not unique to alternative schools.

- How might you adapt your planning if students like Karen or Mario were in your class?
- What are some needs these two students might have and how could you address them in your planning for instruction?

## PLANNING FOR INSTRUCTION

Teachers plan for a year, a semester, a unit, and a lesson with increasing degrees of specificity. Yearly planning is usually sketchy, while unit planning is detailed, and lesson planning is precise. Regardless of the level of detail, plans must always be open to change and revision based on student needs.

### Yearly Planning

Teachers may begin planning for the upcoming year as soon as the current school year ends. As they plan, they consider the relevant academic standards for their subject area. They look at student performance on standardized tests the preceding year and determine how best to prepare students for testing in the coming year. As the academic year begins, they use the first few weeks not only to establish productive learning environments but also to gather information about students' interests, strengths, and weaknesses.

As a first step, teachers review the academic calendar and identify the beginning and ending dates of the semester, holidays, professional development days, and statewide testing periods. They check textbooks and other materials to make sure they have breadth and depth in the curriculum. They review courses of study and curriculum guides and identify additional information they would like to integrate in their classes. They gather information about their students from colleagues and student records. Yearly planning serves as the foundation for semester and unit planning.

### Semester Planning

In the next stage, teachers plan for a semester or a similar division of the academic year. Semesters are approximately 18 weeks long and broken into 9-week grading periods. For each grading period, teachers generally plan several units of instruction. Planning for the semester is more detailed and includes:

- Reviewing state and local mandates to identify the essential content and skills students are to review, learn, and practice;
- Inserting a personal perspective to content and instruction;
- Reviewing course syllabi of previous instructors;
- Identifying the instructional materials to be employed;
- Considering the developmental and individual needs of students;
- Outlining a tentative sequence of content.

This last stage represents an integration of all the steps and leads to the development of the course and units of instruction. For example, a semester plan for Earth Science might look like this:

Course Title: "Learning About the Earth"
  *First Quarter*
    Unit 1. Earth's Structure (2 weeks)
    Unit 2. Earth's Resources (4 weeks)
    Unit 3. Earth History (3 weeks)
  *Second Quarter*
    Unit 4. Meteorology (3 weeks)
    Unit 5. Oceanography (3 weeks)
    Unit 6. Astronomy (3 weeks).

The time frames given in this example are approximate. Teachers would undoubtedly include other learning as they plan their instruction in more detail and as their students acclimate to the culture of their classroom.

## Unit Planning

Unit planning is quite detailed and teachers generally follow a sequence like the one below:

- Outline the concepts, concept clusters, or generalization(s) to be taught;
- Assess the level of difficulty of the content;
- Establish instructional objectives;
- Identify student interests, needs, aptitudes, and experiences;
- Establish performance objectives;
- Sequence learning activities;
- Synchronize student readings with teacher information;
- Identify student activities;
- Map out teaching strategies;
- Select formative and summative forms of assessment.

## AN OUTCOMES-BASED APPROACH TO UNIT PLANNING

One of the benefits of an outcomes-based approach to unit planning is that it provides teachers and students the opportunity look at disciplines from novel perspectives and encourages a more interdisciplinary approach to planning, teaching, and learning. Terri Maloney and Rita Boyd (pseudonyms), who teach language arts in a middle school in central Kentucky, developed the unit "Self Discovery, Self Expression." We will look at their unit to gain an understanding of the standards-based planning process.

Terri and Rita began by brainstorming and agreeing on a unit organizer. The unit organizer sets the context for learning and engages students in exploring an issue or problem. The organizer, usually written in the form of a question, should be open-ended yet focused, nonjudgmental, intellectually challenging, and succinct (Kentucky Department of Education, 1998; Traver, 1998). Terri and Rita settled on the question "Who am I?" as their organizer. Other examples of subject-area guiding questions are: 1. What is a good proof? (Mathematics) 2. How do waves originate? (Physics) 3. What is health? (Health/Physical Education).

Having selected an organizer, Terri and Rita turned to national, state, and local documents to target standards for the unit. Among the standards documents they used were the *National Standards for English Language Arts*, the *Kentucky Learner Goals and Academic Expectations*, the *Core Content for Assessment*, and the *Program of Studies for English I*.

Next, they generated several essential questions. Essential questions narrow the focus of the organizer. They, too, should be open-ended and encourage higher-order thinking and inquiry. These questions should be written in language students can understand because they will be shared with them to direct their learning. Terri and Rita generated four essential questions:

- How have my past experiences sculpted my present sense of self?
- How do I describe myself?
- How can I most accurately express myself through the arts?
- How can I most accurately express myself through writing?

These questions flow naturally from the organizer "Who am I?"

Terri and Rita used all their work up to this point to develop an authentic, culminating performance that would allow students to demonstrate that they could answer the unit's essential questions. They also wanted to give students a role, an authentic purpose, and an authentic audience beyond the teacher. They settled on this project: "Students will create a poster that 'sells' their art work to the Maloney-Boyd Museum." The poster guidelines specified that, over the course of the unit, students would create works of abstract art that expressed who they were. On the poster, students would need to explain their choices about color, shape, and line, and they would need to link their artwork to the personal narratives they had written.

Examples of possible roles, products, purposes, and audiences for culminating performances in other subject areas are: 1. Science: Role–photographer, Product–photo essay, Purpose–document environmental impact of waste disposal, Audience–school open house, 2. Health: Role–athletic trainer, Product–fitness guide, Purpose–recommend healthful diet and exercise practices, Audience–junior varsity athletes. This approach to designing culminating performances encourages students to create authentic products for authentic audiences.

Once Terri and Rita defined the culminating performance, they created a scoring guide of the critical attributes they would look for in the poster. These included the aesthetic qualities of the poster; the extent to which the artwork reflected knowledge of art principles studied in the unit; the extent to which the students made insightful connections between their artwork and personal narrative; and the quality of the writing selected for inclusion on the poster.

As the two teachers identified the skills, knowledge, instructional activities, and formative assessments that would lead to successful culminating performances, Lavonne Caine (a pseudonym), the collaborating special education teacher, identified areas where she could provide help to individuals and instruction that could benefit the whole class but especially the students with Individualized Education Plans (IEPs). The three also identified the resources they would need to accomplish their goals. Terri and Rita had just completed training on WebQuest and were excited about integrating this technology into the unit.

Even at this point, the teachers' work was not complete. They would need to adjust their plan to accommodate unforeseen occurrences, such as computer problems and deadline extensions. And they would certainly learn much from students' culminating performances that would help them revise the unit for the next year.

## LESSON PLANNING

Lesson plans are detailed statements of teacher objectives, student performance objectives, and the procedures that will be followed to attain the stated objectives. The following elements are commonly found in lesson plans:

- Lesson topic/title
- Lesson purpose

- Connections to national, state, and/or local standards
- Teacher objective(s)
- Performance objective(s)
- Relevant content
- Sequence of instruction
- Modifications for meeting special needs
- Assessment procedures
- Instructional materials
- Reflection/evaluation of lesson

Let's look now at how Terri and Rita combined these elements in one lesson plan from the "Self Discovery, Self Expression" Unit–Day Five: Introduction to Abstract Art.

## SAMPLE LESSON PLAN: INTRODUCTION TO ABSTRACT ART

### *Objectives*

1. Students will identify how mood is expressed in the arts.
2. Students will explain how artistic elements are strategically manipulated in order to create mood and other effects.
3. Students will use art terminology to describe works of art
4. Students will create mood in their own works of art.

### *Connections to Kentucky Learner Goals and Academic Expectations*

Goal 1.3: Students will make sense of the various things they observe.

Goal 1.13: Students will make sense of and communicate ideas with visual arts.

Goal 1.14: Students will make sense of and communicate ideas with music.

Goal 2.23: Students will analyze their own and others' artistic products using accepted standards.

Goal 6.3: Students will expand their understanding of existing knowledge by making connections with new knowledge, skills, and experiences.

### *Materials*

Overhead projector          CD player
Transparencies              Colored pencils/markers
Musical selections

## *Procedure*

1. While teacher performs administrative duties, students freewrite: "What do writers, musicians, and other artists have in common?" (5 minutes)
2. Large-group discussion of ideas generated in freewriting. Teacher will connect comments to previous days' activities and to today's objectives. (5 minutes)
3. Students already understand "mood" in popular music. The teacher will play selections from Mazzy Star, the Beach Boys, and Jimi Hendrix (all of which have distinct moods) while students express their understanding of each mood through the following steps.

   a. Write a word/phrase at the top of your paper that captures the mood of the musical excerpt.
   b. Create lines expressive of that mood.
   c. Create shapes/forms expressive of that mood.
   d. Use colors expressive of that mood.

   Collaborating teacher circulates to give individual help and encouragement during this activity. Lead teacher creates abstract drawings along with students. (15 minutes)
4. Students share drawings with a partner. Volunteers share drawings with whole class. (5 minutes)
5. Teacher projects color transparencies of two abstract works of art (e.g., *Red Canna*/Georgia O'Keeffe; *Le Vieux Guitarriste Aveugle*/Pablo Picasso). Teacher models analyzing how an artist manipulates line, color, and form in order to create a mood. Students then independently write analyses of two paintings to share in large-group discussion. (15 minutes)
6. Teacher asks, "What did we learn today about how artists create mood?" Teacher asks students to complete exit slips: "What questions/comments do you have regarding abstract art?" Teacher explains that students will further explore mood in art next week when they begin a WebQuest. (5 minutes)

## *Assessment*

Teacher will assess participation, artistic responses to music, and written analyses of paintings to determine whether students have achieved the objectives.

## A SUBJECT-BASED APPROACH TO UNIT PLANNING

Sandy Eichhorst, a U.S. history teacher living in Champaign, Illinois, uses a subject-based approach to planning.

Sandy begins planning a 2-week unit on "The Roaring Twenties" by concentrating on the first two steps of the planning process: specifying outcomes and identifying student needs. She identifies content that will provide students with opportunities to study the topic in depth, to practice and extend skills, and to explore specific civic values. She also draws on her expertise in political science and interest in the time period, reviews the curriculum materials available, and assesses student needs.

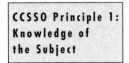

**CCSSO Principle 1: Knowledge of the Subject**

Sandy identifies materials to explore the 1920s from a variety of perspectives. While the textbook is a major tool in her instructional approach, she uses other resources, such as Primary Source, folders she has compiled for particular events and issues in U.S. history. She also consults with her colleagues and identifies community resources that might enhance the unit. She thinks about incorporating the computer game "Decisions, Decisions" (Tom Snyder Productions) to discuss racism and sexism in the 1920s. She will also encourage her students to use Internet search engines to identify sites relevant to this time period.

### Identifying Themes

Sandy decides to focus on the following social studies themes, taken from the curriculum standards of the National Council for the Social Studies (1994): "power, authority, governance," "culture," "science, technology, and society," and "time, continuity, and change." She is considering using "culture" to connect with the other themes. She reasons that, because of the student diversity in her classroom, they will have no difficulty exploring the diverse cultures of the 1920s and similarities between cultures then and now. Second, because adolescents are intensely interested in style, Sandy will introduce the unit by inviting the historian from the community college to assume the character and dress of a flapper and discuss why she has adopted this lifestyle. This will become the introductory activity (hook) to help students make the connection between culture and politics.

### Formulating a Generalization

Sandy will use a generalization to guide the development of the unit. Generalizations are statements with wide applicability that are true or that can be verified on the basis of the evidence provided by the teacher and students. The themes she has selected will be embedded in the generalization. She reflects on the themes, her interests, the availability of resources, and the needs of her students, and then develops the following generalization: *Sandwiched between two wars, the Twenties was a time of political change, a hands-off approach toward business, and a decade of social upheaval and major scientific and technological advancements.*

Sandy is now at the thinking-it-through stage of the planning process: the outlining and sequencing of learning activities and the evaluation of the outcomes of instruction. Given the themes, she will consider at what level of intensity to present the themes, how to show interrelationships among the themes, and how she will assess student learning.

Sandy begins to identify knowledge that will provide for an examination of the themes. She chooses social science and humanities content that will enable students to pursue independently their own intellectual interests in a discipline or across disciplines. Sandy, for example, favors a political interpretation of historical issues and events but is aware that student needs and interests also are part of the planning process. Her professionalism will keep bias to a minimum.

## Selecting Content

After reflecting on her students and the generalization, Sandy selects the knowledge she believes her students should possess about the 1920s. Note that she draws from several social science disciplines.

- The Harding Administration (history and political science)
- President Coolidge's beliefs and policies (political science and economics)
- Factors such as technology, management methods, and credit that played a part in the prosperity of the time period (economics)
- Influence of Henry Ford, a giant of the period (economics and social history)
- Changes in women's lives (sociology, social history, humanities)
- Societal reactions to Prohibition (sociology)
- Media, entertainment, and literature (social history, sociology, English/American literature)
- Examples of fear and intolerance that surfaced during the time period (sociology and social history)

## Instructional Objectives

Next, Sandy allocates days and time to the knowledge statements and assigns instructional objectives to each. She will also develop skeletal lesson plans, including performance objectives. This preliminary plan represents the ideal unit. In reality, she will continue to revise before, during, and after implementation.

Instruction at Sandy's high school occurs in 50-minute periods, a structure that influences the number and nature of the activities she plans for each day. She decides to allocate instructional time as follows:

- Review, overview, and a look at Harding and Coolidge (three class periods)
- Explain why business prospered (two class periods)
- Analyze scientific and technological advancements (two class periods)
- Analyze changes in American lifestyles (one class period)
- Describe the social tension created by the changes in American society (one class period)
- Review and presentation of projects (one class period)

## Teacher Objectives

Sandy will next translate her instructional objectives into teacher objectives. Teacher objectives state the specific content the teacher will present to students. They are crucial in the planning process for two reasons. First, they help sharpen the instructional focus by providing teachers with guideposts that influence subsequent steps in the planning process. Second, they contribute to organized and purposeful learning by providing direction to the teacher and students (Savage, Savage, & Armstrong, 2005).

Sandy identified three teacher objectives to help her achieve her first instructional objective:

***Instructional Objective:*** Review, provide an overview of the unit, and examine the Harding and Coolidge administrations.

- *Day 1 Teacher Objective:* The teacher will determine students' prior knowledge of the 1920s, have a colleague discuss life as a flapper, provide an overview of the unit, and examine two of the political scandals that troubled the Harding administration.
- *Day 2 Teacher Objective:* The teacher will examine President Coolidge's beliefs about government and at least two governmental policies he promoted.
- *Day 3 Teacher Objective:* The teacher will identify specific government legislation that aided the business community and contributed to the prosperity of the decade.

We know *what* content Sandy will teach (i.e., teacher objectives) but we do not know *how* she will present the knowledge (i.e., methodology) or how students will demonstrate a mastery of the content (i.e., performance objectives). We will return to Sandy later to see how she develops performance objectives and selects methods of instruction.

## Student Performance Objectives

Performance objectives communicate the teacher's intent to the learner (Mager, 1997; Marzano, 2006). Performance objectives state what students will do in the classroom, outside the classroom, and outside the school in order to demonstrate learning. They may be modified during instruction as teachers assess the availability of resources, student needs and interests, and other factors influencing instruction.

Now, we return to Sandy's unit outline to develop a set of performance objectives in three domains (knowledge, skills, dispositions). We focus on the 4th and 5th days of the unit, for which the instructional objective is to "Describe Business Practices." Sandy has generated the following performance objectives that are applicable to the whole class:

- *Knowledge*: Students will *apply* what they have learned about life in the 1920s by developing a skit illustrating four behaviors exhibited by the typical city dweller.
- *Skills*: Students will *practice* giving a pep talk speech by acting out the role of Henry Ford exhorting his workers to set new records in automobile production.
- *Dispositions*: Students *are engaged* in constructing a poster illustrating the advantages of buying products using the installment plan.

To summarize, teacher objectives state what specific content the teacher will present. Performance objectives state the knowledge, skills, and dispositions students will use to demonstrate learning.

## Planning for Individual Differences

Some students need additional time or different instructional approaches in order to perform the tasks you outline for the whole class. Some of these students will be brought to your attention by special education faculty or you might identify them through on-going assessment, examining assignments, or simple observation. This semester, Sandy has several students in her U.S. history classes who require special help. Sam and Justin

**CCSSO Principle 3: Diversity**

(pseudonyms) have learning disabilities that make it difficult for them to organize information. Sandy will incorporate graphic organizers into the unit, especially when students need to acquire information from reading or listening. These tools will help all students but will be especially important for Sam and Justin. In addition, she will give them extra assistance as needed. Another student, Pamela (a pseudonym), has a visual impairment that requires instructional modification.

## SAMPLE LESSON PLAN:
## THE ROARING TWENTIES

Provided below is an example of one complete lesson plan from Sandy's unit.

*Topic:* Fear and Intolerance in the 1920s

*Purpose:* Describe how reactions to changes in American culture led to social tension

*Standards:* NCSS (civic ideals and practice, time continuity and change, individual development and change); Illinois Learning Standards 16.B5b: Analyze how U.S. political history has been influenced by the nation's economic, social, and environmental history.

*Teacher Objective:* Introduce examples of fear and intolerance that surfaced in the 1920s.

*Instructional Materials:* Textbook, overhead transparencies and markers, Primary Sources folders containing photos, newspaper accounts, first-person accounts, audiotape, five sets of written directions, and self and group evaluation forms.

*Performance Objective (Knowledge):* Students will describe one example of fear and intolerance in the 1920s, analyze how this example was a reaction to social change, and relate the situation to a contemporary example of fear and intolerance.

*Relevant Content:* The Red Scare, Sacco and Vanzetti, Resurgence of the Ku Klux Klan, Prohibition, Gangland Violence, and the Scopes Trial.

### Instructional Sequence

1. Students respond in writing to the prompt, "Have you ever been accused of doing something wrong that you did not do? What caused this to happen? How did you react?" (5 minutes)

2. Volunteers share responses as teacher writes down key words/ themes on board (e.g., anger, guilt, frustration, guilt by association, unfair). (5 minutes)

3. Teacher asks students to offer examples of unjust accusations, fear, and intolerance from contemporary society (e.g., hate crimes, school shootings, KKK marches) and writes on board. (5 minutes)

4. Transition to 1920s: "Now we will look at how similar events have happened historically." (5 minutes)

5. Teacher divides class into six groups according to six topics listed above as "Relevant Content," and assigns task. Students work in groups. (30 minutes)

6. Begin report, if time. Allow time to collect and put away material. (5 minutes)

***Modifications for Special Needs:*** Teacher assigns mixed-ability groups to help with reading and writing and provides enlarged textbook pages for student with visual impairment.

***Evaluation:*** Presentation will be evaluated for accuracy, clarity, analysis, and insightful connections. Students assess their own and their group's performance using teacher-designed forms.

What is missing at this time is Sandy's reflection on the effectiveness of the lesson after she teaches it.

## SUMMARY

Planning for instruction is challenging, but becomes easier with experience. When teachers are knowledgeable about their students and their subject areas, planning becomes more meaningful and effective, and instruction becomes more enjoyable for both teacher and student. Teachers who are effective planners understand:

- Effective planning begins with a consideration of purposes, knowledge of subject matter, students, curriculum goals, and approaches to teaching a subject area.
- Standards-based approaches to planning may be outcomes-based, subject-based, or student-based.
- Planning units of instruction involves considering the "big ideas" in your subject area together with the characteristics, needs, and interests of students.
- Instructional, teacher, and performance objectives give structure to a unit, help teachers stay focused on outcomes, and let students know what is expected of them.
- Performance objectives can be classified into three domains: knowledge, skills, and dispositions. Objectives in all three domains may not be appropriate for every lesson.
- The goal of teaching key knowledge, skills, and dispositions is to enable students to pursue independently their own intellectual interests.
- Effective lesson plans include modifications for learners with special needs.

### Reflecting on the Standards

- What are your beliefs about the purposes of education and about the purposes of teaching your subject area?
- Are you more of a team planner or would you prefer to work alone? What are some advantages and disadvantages of each approach?
- What are the advantages and disadvantages of writing performance objectives?
- How will you account for student diversity and special needs in your planning?
- What features of the context in which you hope to teach might influence your planning (e.g., a middle school with instructional teams, a high school with block scheduling)?

# CHAPTER 6

# Selecting
# Instructional Materials

Many preservice teachers assume that the instructional materials used in classrooms are appropriate because they were selected by the school district adoption committee, individual teachers, and, in some cases, with the input of representatives of community interest groups. This is true, and in all probability the materials are acceptable for facilitating teaching and learning at a general level. But perhaps, after a more careful look at the textbook you are asked to use, for example, you find that you have some reservations about this educational tool. In this chapter we take a careful look at the textbook and other instructional materials commonly used in the classroom.

The overall purpose of this chapter is related to CCSSO Principle #4: *The teacher understands and uses a variety of instructional strategies to encourage students' development of critical thinking, problem-solving, and performance skills.*

This chapter will focus on enhancing student learning through the use of a variety of resources and materials. It will:

1. Introduce the major tools available for instruction.
2. Present methods of evaluating whether materials are appropriate for particular subject areas, classrooms, and communities.
3. Review standards as instructional tools.

Four subthemes are embedded in the chapter. First, curriculum resources are tools employed by teachers to promote student learning. Second, teachers should choose resources that reflect their educational philosophies and current research on teaching and learning. Third, teachers need to be aware of district expectations of teaching and learning in their particular subject area. Fourth, when carefully selected and employed for their intended purpose, resources are effective in meeting the needs and interests of students and can provide for optimum learning. Specifically, this chapter will help you:

- identify and describe the use of teacher knowledge, textbooks and their ancillary materials, other print resources, community resources, realia, and media;
- use a professional decision-making process to select resources for instruction and to evaluate curricular materials for appropriateness.

## *REFLECTING ON PRACTICE:* JESUS GARCIA– "TEXTBOOKS AS TOOLS FOR BUILDING INSTRUCTION"

In the 1970s, when I was teaching at the fifth-grade level, I had the opportunity to study in Mexico. The intent of the trip was to have U.S. teachers gain a sense of Mexican culture and to observe in secondary classrooms. What I saw in many classrooms I visited was amazingly similar to what I had experienced as a secondary student. Students sat at their desks and the teacher lectured, or students and teachers read from a textbook. While most of the students dutifully followed the teachers' instructions, many appeared disengaged or bored.

In the early 1990s, I was invited to Japan to observe the teaching of social studies in Tokyo secondary schools. The teaching and learning I saw there were quite similar to what I had seen in Mexico. Over the past 25 years, I have visited secondary classrooms in California, Texas, Indiana, Illinois, Kentucky, and Nevada and observed teachers involved in instruction. When I have spoken with some, their conversations focused on the importance of students mastering the curriculum as expressed in the textbook. They said little of the students who appeared to be disconnected from learning.

I like to think of textbooks and other instructional materials as "tools" because this metaphor implies a relationship among teachers, materials, and instructional goals. Effective use depends on one's purpose and ultimately it is the teacher–not the tool–who provides instruction. A tool is simply a means to an end, and the more tools teachers have at their disposal the more variety they provide in their instruction–an essential ingredient when attempting to engage students.

### Questions to Consider

- Reflect on your own school experiences. Describe some of the instructional tools your teachers used.
- What do you recall about textbooks you used and their effectiveness to your overall learning?
- How would schools change if textbooks suddenly disappeared?

## USING MULTIPLE TOOLS FOR MULTIPLE PURPOSES

As you visit schools, walk down the halls and look into the classrooms and identify what resources teachers and students are using. While you will frequently see teacher- and textbook-dominated instruction, you will also see teachers who use the textbook as a reference tool, who integrate additional resources with the textbook, or who do not use a textbook at all.

> **CCSSO Principle 7:**
> **Planning**

The use of a variety of materials is fundamental to effective instruction. First, the use of multiple resources places the responsibility for planning on teachers. It is teachers–not a curriculum guide or textbook–who plan instruction and manipulate resources to meet the envisioned instructional goals. Second, the use of more than one resource encourages teachers to use their knowledge and skills in the planning process. Teachers who develop and hone their planning skills usually avoid becoming dependent on the textbook. Third, employing more than one resource encourages teachers to plan creative instruction that reflects current trends in educational reform, such as cooperative group work and authentic assessment, and addresses student needs. Fourth, as teachers become more successful planners, they become more effective risk-takers, assuming the role of facilitators and guides and giving students responsibility for their own learning. Last, as teachers see students involved in learning and pursuing their own interests, they become reassured, gain confidence, and begin to see the connection between creative instructional planning and productive student behavior.

## TEACHER KNOWLEDGE AS AN INSTRUCTIONAL TOOL

Teachers enter schools with information and experiences and add to this knowledge as they establish themselves in the classroom. The combination of a teacher's knowledge of a subject (content) and knowledge of how to teach the subject to students (pedagogy) is called pedagogical content knowledge (Grossman, 1990; Shulman, 1987). The case of John Foyle (a pseudonym) illustrates how pedagogical content knowledge becomes a powerful instructional tool in the classroom.

> **CCSSO Principle 1:**
> **Knowledge**
> **of Subject**

When John Foyle of Lexington, Kentucky, was in high school, his favorite history teacher introduced him to the United Society of Believers in Christ's Second Appearance (the Shakers). John's fascination with the Shakers and his interest in history and sociology convinced him he should pursue a career teaching secondary social studies. After high school graduation, John enrolled at the University of Illinois. His dream was to return to his hometown and become a social studies teacher. After completing his program of study, he accepted a position teaching world cultures and U.S. history at the high school he had attended.

John's studies at the University of Illinois prepared him well for his teaching assignments. His major consisted of 36 semester hours of U.S. and world history. He minored in sociology, gaining a more in-depth look at the Shakers and worldwide social movements. He also completed 17 semester hours in the other social science disciplines.

Today, John is involved in what he likes most—teaching history, sociology, and world cultures. He has collaborated with other teachers to create an interdisciplinary unit on the Shakers and their role in 19th-century Kentucky. Later in this chapter, we will return to John and other teachers to illustrate how teacher knowledge influences the selection and use of instructional tools.

Like John Foyle, you will graduate from your teacher education program with a wealth of knowledge. Your academic preparation is no less demanding than his. You, too, are successfully completing a number of academic hours and you, too, will possess the necessary content knowledge to teach most of the basic courses in your discipline. When you successfully complete a teacher education program you have earned the right to say that you are on the path to *becoming* an outstanding teacher!

## TEXTBOOKS AS INSTRUCTIONAL TOOLS

Textbooks are the most common instructional tools in the classroom. Because publishers make sure textbooks are aligned with national and state standards, school district officials are more apt to adopt textbooks than other kinds of instructional materials. When you begin your teaching career you may be told that the textbook is your major instructional tool. In this section we describe the student textbook, the teacher's annotated edition (TAE), and ancillary (supplementary) materials accompanying most textbooks.

### Student Textbooks

Student textbooks contain the content students are required to learn about a particular subject at a particular grade level. The content reflects state and district standards and the standards set by the disciplines, and captures the major ideas that appear as questions on standardized tests. Some administrators and teachers see textbooks as conveyors of the official content of an area of study.

Student textbooks contain much more than content. They also are filled with features aimed at helping students master content and skills, and gain a positive disposition toward the subject. A typical chapter in a middle school U.S. history textbook, for example, includes some of the following features: a clear explanation of the chapter's main idea(s) and goals, a timeline, key terms, illustrations, reviews of chapter sections, maps and graphs, contextualized skills teaching, and a chapter summary. At a minimum, as Kellough and Carjuzza (2008) point out, textbooks can provide:

- A base for building higher-order thinking activities (e.g., inquiry discussions and student research) that help to develop critical thinking skills;
- A basis for selecting subject matter that can be used for deciding content emphasis;
- An organization of basic or important content;
- Information about other readings and resources that can enhance the students' learning experiences;
- Previously tested activities and suggestions for learning experiences.

In short, the student textbook contains a wealth of information including content, skills, charts, illustrations, vocabulary, and more to help students learn about a particular subject area.

Textbooks also include strategies for working with English Language Learners and any students who have difficulty reading the text. In social studies textbooks, for example, authors include clues aimed at developing students' abilities to read and learn information from visual sources. Such clues encourage students to: 1. make inferences regarding historical events and situations from visual sources, 2. improve their ability to interpret data presented in visual form, 3. use visuals to improve their comprehension of written text, and 4. improve their ability to think critically about images of historical and current events in the mass media.

> **CCSSO Principle 7:**
> **Planning**
> *and*
> **CCSSO Principle 3:**
> **Adapting Instruction**

Consider how you might use the suggestions below to help students in your subject area.

1. Identify textbooks' reading levels and note the students who are reading below or above grade level.
2. Provide instruction on the purpose for reading and remind students to reflect on purpose prior to reading their text or other materials.
3. Encourage students to use graphic organizers and other techniques to increase reading comprehension.

4. Help students to reduce textbook content to understandable pieces of information.
5. Provide instruction on how to use reading comprehension and study strategies, such as SQ3R, a five-step method (survey, question, read, recite, review).
6. Encourage students to select a reading buddy and use other forms of collaboration.
7. Provide students with study guides of textbook materials and encourage them to identify their own methods of learning textbook content.
8. Provide students with manageable textbook assignments and sufficient time to complete them.
9. Provide copies of textbook pages and illustrate to students ways to learn important key ideas, phrases, and specific information.
10. Model the strategies of an effective reader.

We encourage you to look at the many textbook features aimed at helping all learners master the content.

### Teacher's Annotated Edition (TAE)

The Teacher's Annotated Edition (TAE) is another rich source of information. TAEs can be helpful to both novice and experienced teachers, providing suggestions and information on how to bring breadth and depth to subject area content. For example, *Algebra 2: An Integrated Approach* (Gerver, Carter, Molina, Sgroi, Hansen, & Westegaard, 1998), features introductory essays on team learning, learning styles, multicultural education, portfolios, manipulatives, technology, and a bibliography of suggested readings. Each chapter contains a support system for teachers. Some of the components of the TAE for Chapter 1, "Modeling and Predicting," include:

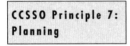

CCSSO Principle 7:
Planning

- chapter theme (Cars and Business)
- class project (build model race cars and hold a car show)
- lesson plan for each topic
- suggested assignments
- technology applications
- math journal prompts
- suggestions for addressing multiple intelligences
- vocabulary notes for English Language Learners
- interdisciplinary connections
- study skills tips

- suggestions for portfolio entries
- suggestions for a culminating performance assessment
- a cumulative review of the chapter (sample problems)
- problems commonly found on standardized tests

Teachers who make wise use of the TAE will find a plethora of ideas, suggestions, and tools that will make the tasks of planning and teaching more manageable and personal.

### Ancillary Materials

Along with a TAE, publishers also offer teachers ancillary (supplementary) materials that can be used with the student textbook. Four types of ancillary materials are generally available: 1. general resources for teachers, such as study guides, lesson plans, visuals, and graphic organizers; 2. resources for addressing student differences, such as materials for English Language Learners, skills practices and challenges, CDs with recorded readings, reteaching resources; 3. ideas about interdisciplinary teaching, such as musical selections and multicultural resources; and 4. test generators.

While developing her unit on the Roaring Twenties, Sandy Eichhorst, the high school teacher introduced in Chapter 5, reviewed the ancillary materials and selected several sources to supplement the textbook's description of the Harlem Renaissance. She found excerpts of Zora Neale Hurston's writings, Langston Hughes's poetry, and paintings done by Lois Mailou Jones, who used African themes in her art. She also found a short historical description of the beginnings of the NAACP (National Association for the Advancement of Colored People). Sandy planned to use a chapter summary written in Spanish (Spanish Language Resources) to help the two English Language Learners who joined her class a few days after the unit was introduced. Next year, with a different group of students, she will use a different set of resources. The key, Mrs. Eichhorst has learned, is to identify specific needs and then look for the appropriate tools.

## OTHER COMMERCIALLY
## PREPARED MATERIALS AS INSTRUCTIONAL TOOLS

Other commercially prepared materials can be supplementary texts, videos on particular themes, and hands-on materials that reinforce textbook content. They are designed to help teachers: 1. provide basic information in all subject areas; 2. enrich the curriculum; 3. address student differences; 4. highlight special topics; and 5. promote an interpretation of a particular topic, event, or personality. These materials are developed and marketed by major and minor publishing companies, as well as professional education organizations, such as the National Council for the Social Studies. A number of nonprofit organizations, such as the Anti-Defamation League and the Southern Poverty Law Center, sell or give away materials that provide alternative views on topics. While some commercially prepared materials can be superficial and extremely biased, many are well prepared and quite useful.

John Foyle, whom you met earlier in this chapter, is looking forward to attending his first National Council for the Social Studies (NCSS) Annual Conference and strolling through the exhibit area where publishing companies display their materials. He will discover materials that contain background information on topics he is teaching; books on strategies and methods of teaching social studies; test banks on the core areas of the social studies–history, geography, civics, and political science; materials aimed at addressing student diversity; posters with historical themes; computer software; and encyclopedias and news magazines.

John will return from the NCSS conference with a multitude of materials. To supplement his DVD collection of biographies, John will consider purchasing two DVDs from Filmic Archives in Botsford, Connecticut: "General Douglas MacArthur: Return of a Legend" and "Attila: The Scourge of God." To sensitize his students to the accomplishments of the physically challenged, he will preview books from Chelsea Curriculum Publications in Broomall, Pennsylvania, describing the accomplishments of men and women "who have found the strength and courage to develop their special talents." Before making a decision to purchase, John will reflect on his goals as a teacher, what he wishes his students to learn, and how he might integrate these materials into the curriculum. Last, he will use an evaluation instrument–like the one we describe later in the chapter–to help him decide whether these materials are a good investment.

## COMMUNITY RESOURCES AS INSTRUCTIONAL TOOLS

All communities possess a wealth of resources, most of which are available to teachers at very little cost. Community resources include field trip locations, resource people (including parents), resource materials, community organizations, and local businesses, industries, and agencies. Making use of community resources enriches the curriculum by bringing the classroom and the community together. Often, districts or schools have documents listing approved community resources.

**CCSSO Principle 3: Adapting Instruction** *and* **CCSSO Principle 10: Community**

A field trip to the local university and a luncheon date with an English professor could provide students in a secondary English class with examples of the universality of themes and examples of their treatment in the college curriculum. A director of the Red Cross could provide a health class with examples of local strategies aimed at combating communicable diseases. A secondary science class could make use of the resources available through a weather bureau or storm center to study the impact of storm-related disasters on the community. Foreign language students could learn the advantages of being bilingual or multilingual by visiting a local self-help organization and observing the language skills of personnel responsible for helping recent immigrants become American citizens.

We must, however, offer a word of caution here. Teachers should follow established procedures when contemplating the use of community resources and adhere to commonsense guidelines. Be sure the community resources you wish to use appear on the district's approved list. If the community resource is not on the list, check with your principal or department chair and obtain written approval. Reflect on your educational goals and objectives and be sure the place you wish to visit, the materials you wish to use, or the speaker you wish to invite is the best source to help you address those objectives. Follow the guidelines listed below to make your connection to the community a successful one:

- Personally preview the community resource before using it.
- Brief speakers on your expectations so that they will be able to address your instructional goals.
- Prepare students to get maximum benefit from the resource. For example, have students prepare questions in advance to address to a guest speaker. Assign specific tasks for students to complete in connection with field trips.
- Have students evaluate the importance of the community resource and contextualize the resource in the unit of study.

## TRADE BOOKS AS INSTRUCTIONAL TOOLS

Trade books are a mainstay resource among those teachers who value a human dimension in their instructional programs. Trade books include works of adolescent and young adult literature, nonfiction, biography and autobiography, poetry, short story, and historical fiction. Teachers use trade books for a number of reasons: to balance the narrow, fact-oriented stance of the textbook; to provide students with an open and interpretive stance on issues, events, and personalities; to engage students; and to promote critical thinking (Bean, Readence, & Baldwin, 2008).

Teachers engaged in collaborative and interdisciplinary teaching find trade books especially useful. At a middle school in suburban Chicago, for example, Jesus observed a social studies teacher and an English language arts teacher agree that along with the U.S. history textbook, the other major readings for a unit on the American Civil War should be the classroom classics *My Brother Sam Is Dead* (Collier & Collier, 2005) and *With Every Drop of Blood* (Collier & Collier, 1994). Both novels are excellent tools for exploring human perspectives in American history. At a high school in Urbana, Illinois, Jesus spoke with a social studies and a science teacher who used the novel *California Blue* (Klass, 1996) to explore both coming of age and environmentalism. An abundance of adolescent and young adult literature is available to teachers. The themes, events, and personalities treated in this literature challenge the imagination.

> **CCSSO Principle 10:**
> **Community**

## MEDIA AS INSTRUCTIONAL TOOLS

Media are the means through which messages are communicated. Young people today absorb more messages from commercial media than they do from textbooks or other school-related printed materials. Media include newspapers, television, radio, film, magazines, comics, music CDs, billboards, and other forms of advertising. Interactive media include CD–ROMs, video games, Internet sites (including blogs), and virtual realities.

> **CCSSO Principle 3:**
> **Adapting Instruction**
> and
> **CCSSO Principle 6:**
> **Effective Communication**

In the classroom, media can be easily integrated into almost any subject area. Film, television, and music clips enhance motivation, enliven a lesson, reinforce content, and help students connect with the curriculum. Many schools subscribe to daily newspapers that are delivered directly to classrooms. Newspapers, radio stations, and magazines around the country and the world have websites where students can read and listen to the news as experienced from many perspectives. Both commercial and public television stations have websites where students can access archives and pursue links to more information. Audiobooks and CDs appeal to many students, especially auditory learners and struggling readers. Students can produce their own instructional materials in the form of videotapes, audiotapes, and CDs. Channel One, a commercial station developed exclusively for schools, is required viewing in some schools. Channel One produces a daily 12-minute news broadcast that includes 2 minutes of advertising, the most controversial feature of its programming. The World Wide Web remains an excellent tool for virtual tours around the world. At no cost it provides teachers with access to museums, national parks, historical landmarks, and locations around the world.

As media producers become ever more sophisticated in their ability to reach and manipulate the public, it is critical that young people possess the media literacy needed to become critical producers and consumers (http://www.medialit.org).

## REALIA AS INSTRUCTIONAL TOOLS

Realia are real objects or reproductions of real objects that can be used in the classrooms. For example, a Spanish teacher who travels to Costa Rica might bring back music, magazines, newspapers, menus, canned goods, fabrics, and many other items that can be used as instructional materials. Similarly, a social studies teacher who travels to Egypt can put together a trunk or suitcase of items that can become instructional materials in a world studies class.

Realia can be any "stuff" you use in the classroom for instructional purposes. Everyday objects can serve to teach concepts and skills: math students can examine patterns in traditional African fabrics; business students can work with tax forms and manuals; and science students can closely observe flowers and leaves. Many creative teachers shop at flea markets, garage sales, and discount stores seeking objects that might bring lessons alive in the classroom.

## EVALUATING INSTRUCTIONAL MATERIALS

The effective teacher seeks to be better informed about how instructional tools are adopted by school districts and the steps they should follow when

| CCSSO Principle 10: |
| Community |

making decisions about what materials to bring into the classroom. Because instructional materials can be expensive and school budgets are often restricted, using rational evaluation procedures can not only help you avoid needless controversy but also guide you to use limited financial resources wisely.

The basic textbook and its ancillary materials are reviewed by a variety of groups before they are adopted at state and local levels. At the state level, board members, teacher leaders, and community representatives have opportunities to comment on materials submitted for adoption. Once materials are adopted, local districts constitute their own committee structure to review materials and to recommend for district adoption. This process is exhaustive, but it effectively eliminates materials that are inappropriate and do not meet state and local standards. Documents produced by the educational community at national and state levels (e.g., national standards or recommendations of blue-ribbon committees) are reviewed informally and may be used to influence local policy and procedures. Some commercially prepared materials and trade books also may be reviewed at the local level.

School officials usually avoid endorsing or adopting materials or documents that are viewed as controversial and that raise the ire of educators, politicians, and community members. If you are not sure about the appropriateness of materials you wish to bring into the classroom, ask yourself these two basic questions:

- Has the material been adopted by the district?
- Have I checked with the department chair or the principal about the appropriateness of the material?

Becoming familiar with these general questions and the evaluation system in place in your school or district is the first step in learning the importance of evaluating material you wish to employ in the classroom. The next step is using an evaluation instrument, such as the ones described below.

A possible first step in the evaluation process is to explore the guidelines established by your subject area's professional organization. For example,

**CCSSO Principle 3: Adapting Instruction and CCSSO Principle 7: Planning**

the National Council of Teachers of English (NCTE, 1996) has published *Guidelines for Selection of Materials in English Language Arts Programs.* This document poses two broad questions relevant to any subject area: 1. What is the connection between the resource and the stated educational objective(s)? and 2. How relevant is the resource to the educational needs of the students? Among other questions teachers need to consider are the following:

- What are the objectives to be met in the unit of study for which the material is intended?
- How will this tool address ethnic, cultural, linguistic, religious, or other relevant characteristics of students?
- What is the need for multiple perspectives on a topic, issue, theme, or genre?

Another instrument, developed by the National Council for the Social Studies (NCSS) and entitled *Curriculum Guidelines for Multicultural Education* (NCSS

Task Force on Ethnic Studies Curriculum Guidelines, 1991), provides educators with guidance in evaluating instructional materials for their multicultural dimensions. These guidelines gauge how well instructional resources meet the goals of multicultural education. While both the NCTE and the NCSS documents could easily be adapted to other subject areas, you should check to see whether your own professional organization has similar guidelines for evaluating instructional materials.

## NATIONAL AND LOCAL
## STANDARDS AS INSTRUCTIONAL TOOLS

Standards documents can be viewed as a major instructional tool for teachers. The standards movement has made the educational community more aware of the importance of selecting instructional

**CCSSO Principle 3:
Adapting Instruction
and
CCSSO Principle 7:
Planning**

materials that are aligned with local, state, and national learning and performance goals. If you are a secondary mathematics teacher teaching Algebra II, for example, national, state, and local standards documents indicate what knowledge and skills you should be teaching, along with examples of how you might teach concepts and classroom scenarios showing students exhibiting understanding of this content. Standards can serve as guideposts in the selection of curriculum materials.

## SUMMARY

Although the textbook is probably the major tool used by middle and high school teachers, it is important to use more than one tool when planning and implementing instruction. Using recognized guidelines to evaluate instructional materials helps teachers make wise financial and instructional decisions. Among the key points to remember are:

- The use of a variety of instructional materials enhances student engagement and learning.
- Instructional materials may be viewed as tools. All tools are most effective when used for their intended purposes, and no single tool is most effective for all purposes.
- When teachers plan using a variety of instructional materials, they gain confidence in their skills and strengthen their roles as instructional leaders.

- One of the most important instructional tools available to a teacher is his or her own knowledge.
- Teachers need to be informed of state and local procedures for adopting and approving instructional materials.
- Many instruments exist to help teachers evaluate the appropriateness of instructional tools.

### Reflecting on the Standards

- How important is the textbook to teaching your subject?
- What kinds of instructional materials do you see yourself using as a teacher and why?
- Do you have a particular interest within your subject area (teacher knowledge) that you will use as an instructional tool?

# CHAPTER 7

# Using Technology
# to Support Learning

Over the past 25 years, we have witnessed remarkable changes in computer-based technology in schools. Some scholars are critical of how schools use or under-use computer-based technology (Cuban 2003). Others note that fundamental changes in how technology is used are necessary in order to maximize the potential of technology to enhance learning.

The purpose of this chapter is to identify essential knowledge and skills beginning teachers must master to meet the standards for educational technology established by the International Society for Technology in Education (ISTE). These standards are the National Educational Technology Standards for Teachers (NETS–T) and they are the organizing focus for this chapter's sections. Each section of the chapter corresponds to one of the five standards developed by the International Society for Technology in Education (ISTE, 2008).

### REFLECTING ON PRACTICE:
### JOSEPH BRAUN–"TEACHING ON THE CUTTING EDGE"

When I began teaching, instructional technology mainly consisted of projecting devices for filmstrips, 16mm films, 35mm slides, and an overhead projector. I thought I was on the cutting edge by integrating the above devices into learning experiences I planned. My students and I looked at slides and 16mm films depicting life in other countries and listened to music to illustrate regional differences in America. Finally, I used a variety of transparencies of maps and primary source documents to make social studies more interesting. For me, instructional technology was hot stuff.

As I began graduate school, middle and secondary schools were creating media centers within the library space to highlight instructional technology including microcomputers, a new development that would eventually eliminate the need for all the aforementioned devices.

By the end of the past millennium, it was commonplace to see teachers and students using the Internet and the World Wide Web. Today teachers can download files of music, images, video recordings, and text from the Internet and develop multimedia shows to accompany the learning experiences they create for students. This is truly "hot stuff" compared to the technology I first used.

### Questions to Consider

- How has the use of educational technology changed over the course of your school experiences?
- What learning experiences with technology have you had outside of schooling?
- How has technology affected how you learn, what you learn, and how you demonstrate what you have learned?

## ISTE STANDARD 1: FACILITATE AND INSPIRE STUDENT LEARNING AND CREATIVITY

As Negroponte (1995) explained, the world used to consist only of atoms but computers changed this: now our world is made of atoms and bits. Bits refers to a numerical encoding system using only 0's and 1's that the computer reads through software. Processed with great rapidity, bits yield enormous amounts of information in files presented as text documents, databases, sound and video recordings, spreadsheets, and images. To become part of the World Wide Web (WWW), these files, along with a file of *hypertext markup language* that becomes a *web page*, are uploaded to a server–a computer working as a gateway to the Internet–with File Transfer Protocol software (FTP). Whether the bits are from a desktop computer, a handheld device, or the Web, teachers have to help engage students in real-world issues and solving authentic problems using digital tools and resources. This section considers strategies for promoting and supporting creative student thinking and inventiveness with technology.

The WebQuest is an Internet-based, inquiry-oriented curriculum model that is designed to inspire students to learn content and use higher-order thinking skills while working cooperatively in small groups. WebQuests contain the following elements: 1. a problem or question; 2. a task that results in a product or summation of learning; 3. a process that includes roles for students; 4. an evaluation component; and 5. credits and information for teachers (http://www.webquest.org). WebQuests vary in length and are most effective when students work in small groups in assigned roles based on the scenario that is described as part of the WebQuest task.

Creating a WebQuest is not as daunting as it might seem. Colleges of education and school districts frequently hold workshops to help teachers acquire these relatively simple skills. What does take some thought is developing a diagram or storyboard for creating a WebQuest. Fortunately, Professor Bernie Dodge, the originator of WebQuest, has created a rich repository of training and support materials that can be found online at http://Webquest. org. The website includes templates for different types of tasks, processes, assessment ideas, background reading on using the WebQuest model, and a large number of examples from K–12 educators all over the country representing every discipline in the curriculum. In addition, this site hosts WebQuests, so you can easily upload your WebQuest and place it on the Web for your students and others to use.

The word cloud (http://www.wordle.net) is an online tool that allows users to create visual representations of a text according to the words most frequently used within it. In a word cloud, higher-frequency words appear in larger font than less commonly used words, whose frequency is represented by the size of the weighted font. Word clouds have many educational applications for inspiring students to think creatively and analytically. For example, Berson and Berson (2009) described how students used word clouds after the 2008 Presidential election to compare Obama's inaugural address to the addresses of former presidents, considering differences in themes and issues raised through word cloud analysis. Key issues from the *Congressional Record* have been used to generate word clouds. Similarly, word clouds can be used to compare the position of one state on an issue to that of another and to track issues over time.

Web-based visualization tools can range from conventional graphs and charts to experimental representations. One tool uses maps to portray geographic data, such as number of breweries or organic farmland, by changing the land size of a state/country to represent the data for that subject, portraying visually both its share of the total and absolute value. Some Web-based sites offering these visualization tools also support an online social network for collaboratively charting and interpreting information. Visualization tools allow students to represent data in unique ways and make thinking visible.

Facilitating student learning through structuring a process for studying art is the focus of REED-LO and its supporting interactive Web-based art tool WAIT (www.waitarttool.com). Developed at the Taubman Museum of Art in Virginia, REED-LO is an acronym for steps to help students interpret a work of art. The steps include Reading, Embracing, Exploring, Deciphering, Locating (the work in its core content), and Opining, or putting forth an opinion as to the work's meaning. Employing the REED-LO process, students use WAIT to create a feedback loop where they can share their interpretations of works of art in the Taubman Museum's permanent collection to which WAIT also provides access (Crawford, Hicks, & Doherty, 2009). WAIT requires students to utilize essential knowledge from core content areas (math, social studies, science, and English) by examining its relationship to a work of art. Students form an interpretation of a piece of art as well as experience an interdisciplinary approach to the arts while employing essential knowledge.

## *ISTE STANDARD 2:* DESIGN AND DEVELOP DIGITAL-AGE LEARNING EXPERIENCES AND ASSESSMENTS

The case of Alena Dryden illustrates how teachers are engaged in designing and implementing digital age learning experiences and assessments. Alena, a middle school science teacher, is part of an interdisciplinary team including social studies, language arts, art, and math teachers. The team works with a group of 80 sixth-grade students from a farming community in Illinois. Alena's team had previously developed interdisciplinary units centered on the year's curricular themes of caring for the environment and world cultures from past to present.

Recently, Alena's team developed a unit on Ancient Egypt. Team planning meetings early in the school year helped the teachers decide upon the goals, objectives, assessments, and activities throughout the year. They used the planning model of "Understanding by Design" (Wiggins & McTighe, 2005) to generate two essential questions guiding the development of the unit: 1. How does where you live affect how you live? 2. How are the lives of Egyptian children today different from those in ancient Egypt? They used the Internet to identify state standards that would be addressed, access potential assessments to evaluate learning, and locate instructional resources.

Alena's team gave considerable thought to managing student learning activities in relation to technology and to monitoring student work (Saye, 1998). Accordingly, they divided their classrooms into different spaces to allow small groups of students to work independently.

| CCSSO Principle 5: |
| Motivation and |
| Management |

Finally, the teachers enlisted the assistance of the media center director for conducting Internet searches as students rotated through this instructional space. The media center director also helped the teachers build a Web page to give parents information about the unit and show how assessment projects addressed state standards. When students were in the media center, the director had visual access to everyone's screen to make sure that students were at appropriate websites, because most adolescents need guidance and a structure that allows them to explore Internet resources safely and efficiently.

The team organized students into small groups who rotated through the learning centers established in each room. One learning center consisted of three classroom computers around which a small group could gather: two Internet-connected computers used for research and one older computer for offline word processing. A second center was equipped with traditional text resources. The computer lab in the media center became a third space where a small group could work with the media center director. In the fourth learning center, a teacher met with the remaining small group to guide and assess their projects through Socratic seminars and other teaching strategies. When the entire group needed to meet, the classroom became a common instructional space for all.

The team also used technology to find appropriate assessments and to identify, locate, and evaluate print and online resources. A multiple-choice/true-false test about Ancient Egypt was generated with commercial software. A simple search on the term *rubric* yielded a plethora of sites that helped the teachers create rubrics they could employ in assessing student learning.

Portfolios are another assessment approach enhanced by technology use, and the teachers generated several ideas for what students might include in a portfolio that reflected their learning about Ancient Egypt. With the video and audio recording capability of computers, student performances, narration, graphics, and music could be incorporated into a powerful vehicle for digitally showcasing what students had learned and could do.

In planning and designing learning experiences with technology, Alena's team needed to address how technologies can accommodate, or in some cases contribute to, students' disabilities. It is important to remember that technology does not always improve the learning of all students. Duhaney and Duhaney (2000) have noted that differentiating instruction to meet the needs of all students, especially exceptional students, requires thoughtful use of media, materials, and technology.

Both Macintosh and Windows operating systems offer accessibility options that can adapt keyboard, screen display, and audio to meet the special needs of students with visual, physical, or auditory learning difficulties. Similarly, modified keyboards are available for students with physical or cognitive disabilities. Speech output communication software allows the user to enter text into a word processing program through the spoken word. Conversely, software can scan text and then reproduce it by reading it aloud to the user. Finally, there is software that converts text into languages other than English. Alena's team reviewed their class lists to identify students who might need some additional support and made arrangements to provide it.

## *ISTE STANDARD 3:*
## MODEL DIGITAL-AGE WORK AND LEARNING

Alena's team illustrates the ways in which teachers model digital-age work and learning. The unit began with an idea found online: embalming a chicken to learn about the Egyptian burial process. Dressed as Egyptian priests and priestesses, the team invited the students into a room designed to look like a pyramid's burial chamber. After playing some Egyptian music, and reading from the Egyptian *Book of the Dead,* the teachers distributed frozen chickens along with instructions on proceeding with the embalming process. For science, students made daily observations and recorded data in spreadsheets and databases as they looked for signs of decay in their embalmed chickens.

> **CCSSO Principle 1:**
> **Knowledge**
> **of Subject**

Alena taught her students how to use a spreadsheet program that was ideal for collecting and managing numerical data on topics related to the essential questions, such as climate conditions, population, caloric intake of children, life expectancy, and other statistics. One curricular trend that incorporates mathematics into other areas of the curriculum is called social mathematics. Social mathematics is an approach to communicating statistics by placing them in a meaningful social context. This is exactly what Alena had in mind as students collected demographic, geographic, and other data described in the case study.

The social studies teacher taught students to use software programs to produce a variety of maps and timelines, as well as presentation software that yields multimedia slideshows showcasing student learning. The art teacher contributed by reviewing the characteristics of a visually appealing presentations using technology. The math teacher found a lesson on the Internet that asked students to prepare a proposal for constructing a pyramid, and through e-mail she put students in touch with a construction contractor who helped them think about what materials they would need to build a pyramid and how to prepare a budget and construction proposal. Students used graphing calculators connected to the teacher's desktop computer to calculate and share projected costs of construction materials.

In addition to all the writing instruction the language arts teacher provided, he helped students use a word processing program to format the layout and incorporate graphics for the newspaper they decided to create. He also taught students criteria to help them evaluate the quality of the information they found online.

The team developed a WebQuest to accompany the unit. The task required students to role play an archaeology team assigned to investigate the suspicious circumstances surrounding the death of King Tutankhamen, the boy king. Members of each team played the following roles: medical examiner, reporter, archaeologist, and historian. Each student visited selected websites and responded to questions such as "How old was King Tut when he died?" "What does the author say regarding the circumstances of his death?" "Is foul play suggested?" Seeking answers to these questions, the students used higher-order thinking skills when analyzing and evaluating the suggested website. As a conclusion, each team wrote a persuasive essay synthesizing the ideas they encountered in their investigation and stating and defending their answer to the question "Was King Tut murdered?" You can view the King Tut WebQuest at http://www.pekin.net/pekin108/wash/webquest/.

Effective teachers model problem solving with databases through a progression of the following tasks: determining information needs, formulating expectations, drawing a tentative conclusion, and presenting the results. Furthermore, they help their students learn by providing them with opportunities to appropriately use cooperative learning, adequate support when maneuvering through the stages of working with databases, promoting higher-order skills, and adjusting instruction for different ability levels.

## *ISTE STANDARD 4:* PROMOTE AND MODEL DIGITAL CITIZENSHIP AND RESPONSIBILITY

The integration of technology into education has raised a host of issues regarding responsible and ethical use. Plagiarism has become a major problem. It is no secret that term papers are available over the Internet for almost any topic; teachers now regularly use the Internet to check whether student work is original. But Mackenzie (2000) has offered three antidotes to the problem of plagiarism.

> **CCSSO Principle 3:**
> **Adapting Instruction**
> *and*
> **CCSSO Principle 9:**
> **Reflection**

First, distinctions in the type of research we ask students to engage in should be established. One level of research is "just the facts," while a more sophisticated level is "other people's ideas." The most significant level, however, is what Mackenzie calls "in my humble opinion." As Alena and her team developed essential questions, they were careful to pose questions that prompted students to construct their own answers, reducing the temptation to look for an easy answer or good essay on the Internet.

Another antidote is to "focus on systematic storage." Students learn to become systematic about note-taking and storage in an electronic database. In addition to the ease of storage and retrieval, when students provide a written justification for each source cited, electronic notes become part of the assessment process. McKenzie also describes a strategy for teaching students to differentiate between ideas they have collected and their own original thinking. McKenzie suggests that the student take electronic notes, using a standard black font for the ideas of others. Then the student selects a different color (such as green) to signify his or her own ideas. The teacher selects yet another font color (such as blue) and responds to the student's notes and ideas about the information. Thus, the note is transformed into a tricolor record of information and the teacher's guidance on what to do next. Of course, the culminating step is to compile the notes into a final project published as part of the multimedia presentation.

Pornography and other objectionable materials abound on the Internet, and the ubiquity of such content raises social, moral, legal, and personal issues. Some schools attempt to limit students' access to inappropriate sites through filtering software. This software looks for key words and then blocks the webpage from the server. Callister and Burbules (2004) point out several problems with this approach. First, the software doesn't work very well: it too often blocks legitimate sites and allows some sites that should be off limits to get through. Second, it is antieducational because it prevents students from accessing materials they might find interesting, important, and relevant to their learning. Finally, there are better solutions. One way is to talk with students about the appropriate use of technology and to have them develop guidelines and possible consequences for when violations occur (Braun, 1999).

The Internet presents another threat to our democratic principles. This involves the right to privacy. Sociologists are exploring how computers are causing us to reevaluate our identities. Social networking sites, such as facebook.com or myspace.com, allow users to be more transparent to online viewers. It seems easy to get to know someone virtually, but no one monitors the accuracy of what one posts. Blogs have become a popular way for individuals to post online regular commentary, graphics, and videos. Social networking sites and blogs are exciting ways to interact over the Internet, but students also need to understand that not everyone with an online presence is who they say they are.

Willard (2003) has described reasons why adolescents may use poor decision making online. These include the lack of face-to-face contact and feedback, disregard of existing social norms and constraints in the new context of cyberspace, and perception of anonymity. Furthermore, continuously accessible environments with wireless technologies, handheld computers, and mobile phones provide growing temptations for misuse, including cheating, plagiarism, and cyberbullying.

The changes and conflicts that technology inevitably brings into our lives are challenging and require new attitudes and strategies for accommodating the relentless pace of technological development. As Kuriloff (2000) has pointed out, educators must prepare students to control, rather than react to, the changes that new technology will bring.

The term *digital divide* describes the fact that many citizens still do not have an adequate level of access to the Internet to engage in a robust civic life. As a teacher, it is your responsibility to prevent a digital divide from developing in your own classroom. All students must learn how to comprehend, generate, and communicate information through computer-based technology. Moving toward a more inclusive environment, schools have created evening computer workshop opportunities and loaned laptop computers to students and some parents (Milone & Saltpepper, 1996).

## ISTE STANDARD 5:
## ENGAGE IN PROFESSIONAL GROWTH AND LEADERSHIP

As a result of the Egyptian unit, one of the students in Alena's class became interested in anthropology. There were, however, no courses of study or instructors locally who could satisfy her eagerness to learn. Arrangements were made for her to participate in an online high school course entitled Introduction to Anthropology. This is one example of how teacher productivity increases with the power of technology as well as an example of how teachers can contribute to the effectiveness, vitality, and renewal of their school and community by providing learning opportunities online and beyond the confines of the classroom.

**CCSSO Principle 6:**
**Communication**
*and*
**CCSSO Principle 9:**
**Reflection**

Online course work offers great promise for extending educational opportunities for students in a variety of forms: supplemental learning to existing curriculum; entire courses, including Advanced Placement credit; and cyber-charter schools where students learn at home. Most online instruction is asynchronous, i.e., students work independently at their own pace. Online instruction may also use streaming video, enabling students to interact in real time with an expert.

Just as online learning presents varied opportunities for students, teachers also use technology for ongoing professional growth. Technology resources can be pivotal in providing the most recent strategies and ideas for classroom applications. Software applications offer additional technology opportunities for teachers to create curriculum materials that enhance the learning experiences they provide. PowerPoint® and interactive whiteboards are examples of multimedia software. Interactive whiteboards capture writing electronically, allowing users to print or save what has been written. Digital presentations can also be shared on a server, posted on a webpage or blog for students (or other teachers) to download.

Facebook, twitter, wiki, and ning are all new names for software on websites leading an explosive growth of social networking among teachers. Such sites allow teachers to blog, and to post videos, images, and resources for teaching as well as find others who have similar interests in their discipline or how they teach. Moreover, teachers can demonstrate leadership by using social networking sites as a way to promote professional growth for others.

## SUMMARY

This chapter has described the standards that many states have adopted to gauge the instructional effectiveness of teachers when using technology. Among the key points to remember are:

- Web-based visualization tools allow students to learn and express ideas in unique ways.
- Teachers are responsible for teaching students online searching skills and critical thinking skills for evaluating the authenticity, accuracy, and relevance of the results of websites identified by a search.
- Technology demands that teachers think through classroom management and accessibility issues.
- WebQuest is a tool for online inquiry.
- Databases and spreadsheets are tools used to organize and explore relationships among data and can be used for assessment.
- As technology becomes integral to teaching and learning in the 21st century, social (e.g., cyberbullying), ethical (e.g., the digital divide), and legal (e.g., plagiarism) issues have arisen that were not present in schools before.
- Technology provides a powerful tool for teacher learning and networking.

***Reflecting on the Standards.*** How can technology support your purposes as a teacher? With respect to the subject matter(s) you will be teaching, how will you use technology in your first year of teaching?

- How can you as a teacher use technology to address equity issues in your subject area?
- What social, ethical, legal, and human issues regarding technology are likely to arise in your subject area?

# CHAPTER 8

# Implementing Instruction:
# Teacher-Directed Strategies

Reflect on your own educational experiences. Do you recall teachers whose teaching methods inspired you and whom you hope one day to emulate? Perhaps these teachers were great lecturers, led lively discussions, or assigned projects that interested and engrossed you. In this chapter you will be introduced to a set of instructional strategies we refer to as *teacher-directed*, because these methods usually place teachers at center stage. These include lecture, questioning, leading discussions, and other strategies for presenting content. The next chapter will introduce you to a set of instructional strategies we call *student-centered*, because they give students more responsibility to direct their own learning. These include project- or problem-based learning and small group tasks.

The overall purpose of this chapter is related to CCSSO Principle #4: *The teacher understands and uses a variety of instructional strategies to encourage students' development of critical thinking, problem solving, and performance skills.*

Specifically, this chapter will help you:

- Understand how and when to implement teacher-directed techniques, including direct instruction, mastery learning, lecture, questioning, and whole-group discussion;
- Develop strategies for presenting and representing concepts in your subject area and for helping students access and organize knowledge;
- Vary your role in the instructional process in relation to the content and purposes of instruction and student needs.

Good teachers possess a wide repertoire of techniques and choose instructional strategies based on many criteria, including their own familiarity and comfort with particular techniques; the academic, social, and personal goals they set for their students; the effectiveness of certain strategies with specific groups and individuals; the changing learning needs of students; and the availability of resources such as time, space, and materials.

*REFLECTING ON PRACTICE:*
**LIZ SPALDING–"MY LEARNING STYLE ODYSSEY, PART I"**

When I was teaching English and foreign languages to middle and high school students, my repertoire of instructional strategies was limited. Like many other English teachers at that time, I believed that knowledge of the parts of speech, the parts of a sentence, and various rules of usage would help my students become better writers and speakers. With the aid of a textbook, worksheets, the chalkboard, and the overhead projector, I would explain a grammatical construction such as prepositional phrases, review examples with the class, call on students to complete some exercises aloud, and then assign individual exercises to be begun in class and finished as homework. The next day, we would check and grade the exercises. At some point, students would take a quiz or test on the material covered. Regardless of students' scores, I forged ahead to the next topic. Two weeks later, if I asked students to vary sentence beginnings by using prepositional phrases, most reacted with blank stares.

At the same time, I was teaching French quite differently, using methods I had learned in my subject-area methods class. When we studied prepositional phrases in French, students would physically respond to oral commands ("Put the pencil on the floor"). They would give oral commands using prepositions in a game of "Simon Says" ("Simon says, 'Walk toward the door'"). I would place familiar objects in unusual places around the classroom and have students tell me what was out of place ("The clock is on the floor"). As homework, students would write descriptions of their bedrooms in French, using at least five different prepositional phrases ("My jeans are under the bed"). The next day, they might read their descriptions to a partner who would sketch a picture of the bedroom based on the written description. In spite of (or because of) the fact that they were actually having fun, my French students seemed to understand prepositional phrases much better than my English students.

As I gained experience, I realized that active involvement and application of knowledge to real-world problems are key to learning in all content areas. I wasn't really *teaching* my English students about prepositional phrases; I was simply *assigning* tasks and hoping that they would learn. My French students were more successful because they were using their knowledge for authentic purposes and practicing the language in a variety of modes (i.e., seeing, hearing, speaking, doing).

### Questions to Consider

• What were the predominant instructional strategies you experienced in schooling?

- What instructional strategies have proven most effective for your own learning? Least effective? Why?
- What instructional strategies have you practiced and observed in your teacher education program?

## STANDARDS FOR
## AUTHENTIC INTELLECTUAL ACHIEVEMENT

Students learn best when they are actively constructing meaning based in their own experience rather than simply absorbing and reproducing knowledge (Newmann, Marks, & Gamoran, 1996). *Authentic intellectual achievement* results when students engage in constructing meaning. The term *authentic* means genuine or realistic. Authentic tasks enable students to apply skills and knowledge in a real-world context.

CCSSO Principle 2:
Learning and
Human Development

Authentic intellectual achievement meets three criteria (Newmann, Marks, & Gamoran, 1996). The first is *construction of knowledge.* Such activities as labeling body parts, defining terms, or matching authors to works may be necessary precursors to knowledge construction, but they are not examples of knowledge construction. Students construct knowledge when they use words or symbols to write or speak about their learning, make things such as machines or movies, and perform for audiences. The second criterion is *disciplined inquiry.* Disciplined inquiry means that individuals build on a prior knowledge base from one or more fields. The knowledge base may include facts, specialized terminology, theories, concepts, and conventions for conducting investigations in the discipline. Disciplined inquiry aims to develop in-depth understanding, which requires more than knowing lots of details about a topic. Finally, authentic intellectual achievement has *value beyond school.* Activities have value beyond school when they satisfy "aesthetic, utilitarian, or personal" purposes, such as speaking a foreign language, creating a painting, or writing a letter to the editor (p. 284).

## AUTHENTIC AND EFFECTIVE PEDAGOGY

Pedagogy is the art of teaching. Authentic pedagogy has the following characteristics:

- It involves students in *higher-order thinking* by asking them to synthesize, generalize, explain, hypothesize, or arrive at conclusions that produce new meanings.

- It engages students in *substantive conversations* about subject matter with the teacher and/or their peers in a way that builds an improved understanding of ideas or topics.
- It helps students develop *depth of knowledge* by addressing the central ideas of a topic or discipline with enough thoroughness so that they can explore connections and produce complex understandings.
- It enables students to *make connections between academic knowledge and the world beyond the classroom* (Newmann, Marks, & Gamoran, 1996).

The standards for authentic pedagogy described above are important for all learners, but it is especially important that students from diverse backgrounds have teachers who use these and other linguistically and culturally appropriate methods. Gay (2002) defined *culturally responsive teaching* as "using the cultural characteristics, experiences, and perspectives of ethnically diverse students as conduits for teaching them more effectively" (p. 106). Culturally responsive teaching methods require demonstrating cultural caring and building a learning community, becoming informed about communication styles of different ethnic groups and using the information to guide communication in the classroom, matching instructional techniques to the learning styles of diverse students, and using culturally relevant examples to teach knowledge and skills. In addition, English Language Learners need numerous opportunities to develop their language skills across the curriculum (Echevarria & Goldenberg, 1999).

> **CCSSO Principle 3:**
> **Adapting Strategies**

Authentic pedagogy does not preclude the use of drill, repetition, or memorization. Traditional forms of schoolwork have their place. The point is to "keep authentic achievement clearly in view as a valued end" (Newmann, Marks, & Gamoran, 1996, p. 288).

## CREATING A CLASSROOM COMMUNITY

Your efforts to implement authentic and effective pedagogy will be much more successful if you make time to create and sustain a sense of classroom community in which all members take responsibility for the good of the group and which teaches personal, ethical, and social knowledge and skills as well as academic ones (Gay, 2002).

> **CCSSO Principle 5:**
> **Motivation and**
> **Management**

Many teachers dedicate the first few weeks of the school year to community building in the context of learning content and classroom procedures. Icebreakers and team-building activities are relatively easy to find, create, and implement (Silberman, 1996). You can create surveys to find out about students' interests and interests in your subject, and the results become tools not only for building classroom community but also for building relationships with individual students and for finding keys to help them connect to school learning (Tomlinson, 2001).

## DIRECT INSTRUCTION

*Direct instruction* is an approach that is appropriate for teaching well-structured tasks. Well-structured tasks are those that can "be broken down into a fixed sequence of subtasks and steps that consistently lead to the same goal" (Rosenshine, 1995, p. 265). Examples are mathematical computations, map skills, or operating a computer. Reading comprehension, writing, and study skills are examples of less structured tasks for which direct instruction may not be appropriate. Many commercial programs use a direct instruction model and claim to be especially effective with students who have not mastered grade-level skills (Kozioff, La Nunziata, Cowardin, & Besselieu, 2001). A direct instruction lesson generally follows the outline below.

- *Review* homework, previous learning, prerequisite skills and knowledge.
- *Presentation* of lesson goals and new material in small steps. Teacher models procedures, provides positive and negative examples, uses clear language, and checks for student understanding.
- *Guided practice* during which all students respond and receive feedback. Students continue practicing until fluent in the skill.
- *Corrections and feedback* from teacher so that students do not practice errors and misconceptions. Teacher reteaches materials when necessary.
- *Independent practice* during which students practice skill on their own in class or as homework.
- *Weekly and monthly reviews* insure retention and continued mastery (Rosenshine, 1995).

## MASTERY LEARNING

Like direct instruction, mastery learning is based on the principle that *all* students can learn, given time, practice, feedback, and resources (Bloom, Madaus, & Hastings, 1981; Kozioff et al., 2001). A teacher who uses mastery learning specifies student objectives, teaches the concepts or skills, and assesses student attainment of the objectives. After students receive feedback on their performance, the teacher provides additional time or resources for the students who have not yet demonstrated mastery, often stated as a particular level (e.g., 80% correct). Students who have attained this level move on to the next unit or complete enrichment activities, while the students who need more time get it. After reteaching, the teacher retests. Theoretically, this cycle goes on until all students have achieved mastery. Implementing mastery learning requires in-depth knowledge of content, students, and resources, as well as excellent classroom management skills (Walberg & Paik, 2004).

## LECTURE

Lecture remains a widely used strategy for presenting and explaining information to students and is especially appropriate in the following situations.

- When the objective is to present information that is not readily available from another source, is original, or must be integrated from different sources;
- When the objective is to arouse interest in the subject;
- When the information needs to be summarized or synthesized (following discussion or inquiry);
- When the teacher wants to present alternate points of view or to clarify issues in preparation for discussion;
- When the information is not intended for long-term retention or memorization (Chuska, 1995).

Lecture is based on the assumption that all students learn equally well by listening, and thus it may not address students' diverse learning styles. In addition, because lecture places the teacher at center stage, students can easily become disengaged or mindlessly copy facts without processing them at higher levels. Lecture, however, is still widely regarded as the most efficient means of conveying information to large numbers of people at one time. What can you do to ensure that students get the most out of a lecture? Your lecture presentations need to be succinct, clear, and interactive.

In a succinct lecture, the teacher: 1. identifies goals for student learning; 2. monitors and signals progress toward the goals; 3. uses demonstrations to provide alternative representation of concepts, link concepts, and identify examples and non-examples of concepts; 4. links new concepts to ones already familiar to students and builds on their prior knowledge (Perkins, 1995).

When giving presentations, teachers attend to clarity by:

- Determining how the information to be learned links to students' current knowledge, including areas of potential confusion or misconceptions;
- Organizing materials to promote student understanding;
- Arranging the information in a logical way that is appropriate to the content and the learners.
- Explaining principles and relating them to facts through examples;
- Using effective presentation skills including voice modulation, appropriate pacing, nonverbal communication, and visual aids (Good & Brophy, 2002).

Interaction keeps students involved in lecture presentations (Harmin & Toth, 2006). Following are examples of some of the many strategies you can use to involve students throughout a presentation of information.

- *All Write.* At appropriate intervals (e.g., 3–5 minutes), teacher asks all students to jot down key ideas they have heard and/or questions they have about material.
- *Pair-Share.* Students form pairs and share summaries of what they have heard.
- *Summary.* Teacher summarizes key points of presentation.
- *Attentive Discussion.* Teacher asks class to share ideas, reactions, and questions.
- *Outcome Sentences.* Individually, students write a few sentences describing key learning, asking for clarification, raising new questions. If handed in to teacher, these are a quick way to assess learning.
- *Whip Around, Pass Option.* Students take turns making a statement, "I learned . . ." Students have the option of saying, "I pass . . ." (but let them know you'll come back to them later or another day).

## HELPING STUDENTS DEVELOP, PROCESS, AND ORGANIZE KNOWLEDGE

Research on *cognitive processing*, the systems we use to store and retrieve information, has demonstrated how important it is for teachers to help students develop a "well-connected body of accessible knowledge" (Rosenshine, 1995, p. 262). The instructional strategies described in this section are intended to help students build strong networks of knowledge.

## Advance Organizers

Students often need help organizing and understanding the information that is presented to them through expository teaching (i.e., presenting, explaining, and discussing material). Advance organizers help introduce content to be studied by bridging the gap between what the learner already knows and what he needs to know (Ausubel, 2000). Advance organizers also help students learn more effectively because they know what to expect.

Organizers may take different forms, such as a concept or a statement of a relationship. For example, a teacher might use the concept of *social stratification* as an advance organizer for a lesson on India (Joyce, Weil, & Calhoun, 2004). The teacher might ask students what they already know about social stratification in the community or in the school and perhaps hypothesize about the social status of people from various cultures depicted in photographs.

Examples of other advance organizers include note-taking guides, demonstrations, film clips, models, maps, and magazines (Story, 1998). Regardless of the form it takes, the advance organizer should be based on a major concept or generalization in your discipline and prepare the students' minds for learning.

## Graphic Organizers

Graphic organizers are visual representations of knowledge, concepts, or ideas. They have been extensively studied and found to be effective aids to learning because they provide ways to represent and organize one's thoughts and knowledge visually (Rock, 2004). One example of a graphic organizer is the Venn diagram, composed of intersecting circles, which is useful for helping students identify similarities and differences between or among people, places, things, and ideas. These *tools for thought* may be especially helpful for students who struggle with academic tasks for a variety of reasons (Burke, 2002).

Teachers can create graphic organizers for students or students can create their own. Access to drawing software and online clip art makes graphic organizers more attractive and easier to create than ever before. At the same time, much can be accomplished with plain paper and markers.

## HELPING STUDENTS DEVELOP THINKING SKILLS

Deductive reasoning is the type of reasoning most closely associated with direct instruction and presentation of information. *Deductive teaching* moves from the general to the specific. A teacher using a deductive approach usually presents a general concept, defines it, and presents examples of it. *Inductive teaching* moves from the specific to the general. A teacher using an inductive approach presents examples or nonexamples, cases, or problems from which students induce the general principle involved.

Whether a teacher uses a deductive or an inductive approach, the goal is for students to gain knowledge. Knowledge can take several different forms. *Procedural knowledge* (knowing how) refers to understanding the symbols, rules, and steps involved in accomplishing a task. These are the skills we teach our students within our subjects, such as conducting a science experiment or, given the longitude and latitude of Mexico City, locating it on a map. *Content, or factual knowledge* (knowing that), requires students to commit information to memory or know how to look it up in an appropriate reference. "The Louvre is a world-renowned art museum located in Paris, the capital of France" is an example of content knowledge. *Conceptual knowledge* involves understanding of and the relationships among key terms or ideas imbedded in any subject matter. A student must understand the concepts of a museum and a capital in order to understand the meaning and significance of the Louvre and Paris.

## Concept Attainment

Teachers use concepts as organizing frameworks that provide a meaningful focus for specific subject matter and information that is being studied. Helping students build accurate conceptual constructs so related things are placed in the correct intellectual category is a hallmark of good teaching (Jarolimek, 1991). When we teach concepts, we are trying to help students build mental images that do not exist in nature but instead are human constructions. For example, zoologists (and others) have agreed that mammals (a concept) have certain attributes and that reptiles (a concept) have other attributes, although both do share some attributes in common. It is the differing attributes that make it possible to correctly categorize a cat or a cobra, which are single, specific examples that exist in nature.

Below is a seven-step strategy for teaching concepts.

1. Students study three or four examples of the concept to be formed.
2. Students identify differences among the examples.
3. Students identify similarities among the examples.
4. Students summarize the similarities into a defining statement that incorporates the critical attributes of the concept. (Now the concept has been constructed.)

5.  Students label the concept. (Now it has been named with terms that are meaningful to students.)
6.  Students learn the conventional label for the concept (what we've agreed to call it).
7.  Students refine and elaborate the concept by examining new examples, distinguishing examples from nonexamples, creating/ finding new examples, correcting nonexamples (Parker, 1988).

## Concept Maps

Concept maps help students "visualize how major ideas are related to their own prior knowledge, subordinate ideas, and associated ideas from other topic areas" (Kinchin, 2000, p. 61). Teacher-created concept maps can be used as advance organizers. Students' concept maps can reflect the breadth, depth, and complexity of their understanding of a topic as well as their misunderstanding. An example of a concept map from biology appears in Figure 8.1.

**FIGURE 8.1. Concept Map from Biology**

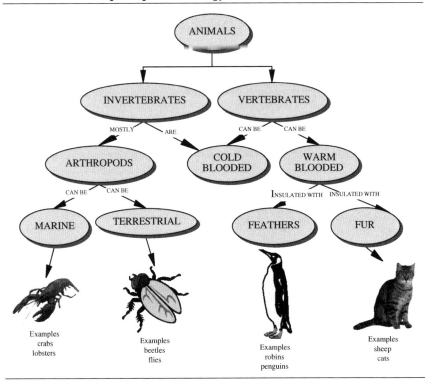

## ENCOURAGING HIGHER-ORDER
## THINKING THROUGH QUESTIONS

Teachers may ask as many as 300–400 questions per day (Wilen, 1991). While most teachers hope that their questions will stimulate higher-order and creative thinking in students, many questions fall short of this goal. As you plan for and implement instruction, you need to consider the kinds of questions you ask as well as how you ask them.

### Kinds of Questions

Many classroom questions resemble quiz show items. Students are asked to answer questions with content or factual knowledge. Facts are important, but being able to put facts to use is more important.

Bloom's (1956) taxonomy of educational objectives has been used to guide the development of student objectives in the cognitive domain. It has also been used to classify the questions teachers ask according to the intellectual operation required to answer: knowledge, comprehension, application, analysis, synthesis, and evaluation. Table 8.1 suggests sample verbs and question stems to correspond to each level of Bloom's taxonomy.

Questions can also be divided into two broad categories: convergent and divergent. *Convergent questions* are used to determine basic knowledge and require responses to converge upon a single or simple answer. *Divergent questions* are used to engage students in critical thinking and encourage responses to branch out in various directions (Wilen, 1991). Models of questioning such as Bloom's and Wilen's provide useful frameworks for planning and analyzing the questions you might ask in the classroom. You should also explore other models for planning thought-provoking and challenging questions (Christenbury & Kelly, 1983; Chuska, 1995; Marzano, Pickering, & Pollock, 2001).

### Questioning Techniques

Planning good questions is one aspect of effective teaching. Knowing how and when to ask them is another. In practice, you will soon discover a myriad of questions about questioning. Some of them can only be answered through experience and getting to know your students. By watching your students as they interact in discussion, by listening to their responses, and by being mindful of your own actions, you will develop insight into the best ways to respond to the variety of situations that arise in the course of discussions. Following are some techniques that can help you be a better questioner in most classroom settings.

**CCSSO Principle 6:
Effective
Communication**

**TABLE 8.1. Types of Questions Based on Bloom's Taxonomy**

| Taxonomy Level | Sample Verbs | Sample Question Stems |
|---|---|---|
| Knowledge | List, describe, name | Who was it that . . . ? <br> What happened when . . . ? <br> Who said . . . ? |
| Comprehension | Restate, explain, outline | What was the main idea . . . ? <br> Can you define . . . ? <br> In your own words . . . ? |
| Application | Solve, use, illustrate | Could this have happened in . . . ? <br> Can you apply this information to some experience of your own? <br> What questions would you ask of . . . ? |
| Analysis | Analyze, categorize, explain | What was the underlying theme of . . . ? <br> How is . . . similar to . . . ? <br> What are some of the problems with . . . ? |
| Synthesis | Create, design, propose | What would happen if , , , ? <br> How many ways can you . . . ? <br> If you could devise your own solution . . . ? |
| Evaluation | Justify, prioritize, determine | Is ___ a good or bad thing? <br> How effective was . . . ? <br> Is there a better solution to . . . ? |

***Wait time.*** The time that elapses between the moment you finish asking a question and the moment a student volunteers an answer may seem like an eternity. But, in fact, researchers have shown that many teachers wait less than 1 second after asking a question before reacting in some way, e.g., answering the question, restating it, asking another question (Wilen, 1991). Rowe (1986) found that when teachers increase "Wait time one" to 3 seconds or longer, both the quality and quantity of students' responses improve. "Wait time two" occurs after a student responds. Again, Rowe found that when teachers increased wait time two to 3 seconds or longer, students were more likely to elaborate and produce higher-quality responses. "Wait time three" is the pause that occurs between student-to-student dialogue (Swift, Gooding, & Swift, 1988). Teaching yourself and your students to wait just a few seconds before speaking can enhance the quality of talk in your classroom.

*Verbal Feedback.* Costa (1990) has categorized types of teachers' responses to students during questioning and discussion into those that close down discussion and those that promote it. Teacher responses that close down discussion are criticism, put-downs, and praise. Costa and other researchers have found that indiscriminate use of praise encourages students to be dependent on others for their ideas; when praise is reduced, students tend to experiment and speculate more in their responses.

*Accepting responses* promote discussion. Accepting responses are those that acknowledge but do not place a value judgment on students' contributions. *Passive acceptance* includes nodding the head, recording the student's response on a chart, or uttering a neutral response such as "Um-hmm" or "That's one possibility." *Active acceptance* includes paraphrasing, summarizing, or building upon a student's response. *Empathic acceptance* accepts the feelings as well as the ideas behind a response. Often, *probing* or asking a follow-up question can help clarify and extend a student's thinking: "You said you thought the character's decision was stupid. Could you tell us a little bit more about why you think so?" Sometimes, you may want to *redirect* a question that you have asked: "Mike has told us what he thinks of the character's decision. Claire, what do you think?"

*Employing Equitable Patterns of Questioning.* As you observe and teach in classrooms, you will discover that frequently only a small number of students consistently volunteer to answer questions and tend to dominate discussion. Furthermore, teachers, albeit unconsciously, are inclined to call on some students consistently and to overlook others. In addition to becoming aware of your own questioning patterns and to getting feedback from observers, there are several strategies you can employ to distribute questions more equitably.

The Whip Around/Pass activity described on page 115 encourages every student to participate in a relatively low-risk situation. Another strategy is to pose a question, have all students write down the answer, and then call for responses or have students share responses with a partner. Some teachers write students' names on index cards or popsicle sticks and pull them randomly to call on students. Good teachers vary their questioning strategies systematically to ensure that all students have the opportunity to participate.

## Sociocultural Differences and Teacher Questioning

As recent research has focused on the sociocultural features of classroom talk, more and more teachers are realizing that no model of questioning fits all contexts. Styles of verbal and nonverbal communication are influenced and shaped by language, culture, ethnicity, gender, and social class. In order to ask good questions and understand students' responses, teachers need to take into account and build upon the patterns of verbal interaction found in students' home communities (Delpit, 1995; Echevarria & Goldenberg, 1999; Gay, 2002; Heath, 1983).

## TEACHER-DIRECTED DISCUSSION

*Authentic discussions* are "dialogically-oriented classroom interactions where participants present and consider multiple perspectives and often use others' input in constructing their contributions" (Hadjioannou, 2007, p. 370). *Recitations*, on the other hand, are characterized by a pattern of teacher question-student response-teacher reaction. Recitation is used to determine students' command of factual knowledge, a prerequisite for and often a prelude to discussion.

Ideally, discussion helps students go beyond acquiring information and enables them to apply knowledge and skills. It helps them learn and practice interpersonal and verbal skills required for participation in a democracy. Perhaps most important, in an increasingly diverse society and world, discussion is the foundation for building knowledge and solutions to complex political, ethical, and environmental problems (Michaels, O'Connor, & Resnick, 2008).

The teacher's role in discussion is as the leader of the classroom community who provides the class with both a physical and social environment conducive to helping students "take substantial social risks, offer tentative contributions, and state controversial opinions" (Hadjioannou, 2007, p. 385).

### Accountable Talk

Michaels, O'Connor, and Resnick (2008) have studied discussion practices in classrooms for over 15 years. They have found that discussions characterized by *accountable talk* promote equity and access to academic learning and result in academic achievement for diverse populations of students. Accountable talk holds students *accountable to the learning community*. That is, talk in the classroom requires listening to and building upon the contributions of others. Participants provide reasons for why they agree or disagree and offer and ask for elaboration. *Accountability to standards of reasoning* requires students to make logical connections and draw reasonable conclusions. *Accountability to knowledge* requires that speakers make an effort to get their facts right and to make explicit the evidence behind their claims. Because not all students come from homes or cultures where accountable talk is a value, it may take a teacher many months to build a classroom community in which authentic discussions take place.

### Improving Metacognitive Skills Through Discussion

*Metacognition* is the awareness of one's own thinking processes. Students who are aware of and can monitor their own thinking processes have more control over their learning. A number of strategies exist for helping students develop and use meta-cognitive skills in discussion. *Strategy planning* consists of taking time before a discussion to establish with students criteria for effective participation and afterward to debrief as a class on the discussion process. Students can: 1. use journals to record their thoughts and questions during discussion and keep track of their changing ideas over time; 2. volunteer to map for the class on chart paper or overhead the concepts and subconcepts that emerge during the discussion; and 3. use a set of predetermined questions to monitor their thinking during discussion (e.g., Does this discussion make sense? How does this relate to what I already know? What are this person's basic assumptions?).

> **CCSSO Principle 2:**
> **Learning and**
> **Human Development**

## SUMMARY

This chapter presented a sampling of teacher-directed strategies that help to foster authentic intellectual achievement. When selecting instructional strategies, you should consider your own teaching style, the characteristics of your students, educational goals, and the appropriateness of the strategy for the content or processes you are teaching. No single strategy is always effective for all students. Among the key points to remember are:

- Creating a classroom community is a prerequisite to authentic learning.
- Effective instructional strategies are selected for specific purposes and implemented with student learning needs and characteristics in mind.

- Teacher-directed strategies include direct instruction, mastery learning, and lecture.
- Preparing good questions and using good questioning techniques are skills that can be learned and refined.
- Authentic discussions require higher-order thinking and hold students accountable for their talk.

### Reflecting on the Standards

- Which of the instructional strategies presented in this chapter are you most likely to use? Why?
- Which of the standards for authentic intellectual achievement and pedagogy are most important for your subject area?
- How can what you learn from students help you design and adapt instruction?
- Which teacher role do you find most appealing: instructor, facilitator, coach, audience? In your subject area, when would you assume each role?

## CHAPTER 9

# Implementing Instruction: Student-Centered Strategies

This chapter will introduce you to a set of instructional strategies we call *student-centered*, because they give students more responsibility to direct their own learning. Instructional strategies are student-centered when students actively engage in small-group work, rotate through learning centers, dramatize critical moments in history, or role-play a political debate. For most of the instructional strategies discussed in this chapter, the teacher plays the role of the guide on the side.

The overall purpose of this chapter is related to CCSSO Principle #4: *The teacher understands and uses a variety of instructional strategies to encourage students' development of critical thinking, problem solving, and performance skills.*

Specifically, this chapter will help you:

- Design instruction to address individual differences through differentiated instruction;
- Understand how and when to implement small-group work, student-led discussion, and student-to-student teaching;
- Individualize instruction through learning centers, activity packets, and contracts;
- Provide learning experiences that help students make connections to the world beyond the classroom through role-playing, simulation, drama, and problem-based learning.

Excellent teachers have mastered a repertoire of both teacher-directed and student-centered strategies and choose instructional strategies according to their learning goals.

## *REFLECTING ON PRACTICE:*
## LIZ SPALDING–"MY LEARNING STYLE ODYSSEY, PART II"

As I gained experience as a teacher and added to my repertoire of instructional strategies, I relied more and more frequently on student-centered methods of instruction. For example, while reading *Wuthering Heights* each student selected a character to follow throughout the novel. Students kept journals about their characters and periodically wrote entries assuming that persona. The school counselor helped me administer and interpret the results of personality tests that each student completed as Heathcliff, Catherine, Edgar, Isabella, or another of the novel's characters. As a final project, students role-played family counseling sessions for the various relationship groups in the book.

Eventually, I left high school teaching and, while exploring other career options, I completed learning style and personality type inventories. I discovered that I learned best from hands-on activities and preferred unstructured learning situations in which I have some freedom to choose what to learn, how to learn, and how to show what I've learned. Only then did I realize that my teaching style reflected my learning style. For example, I felt most comfortable when my students were role-playing characters in literature, working in groups to create visual representations of people and places, or ordering from a menu in my classroom French cafe. For years, I had assumed that, like me, my students would relish the opportunity to be creative and to demonstrate originality. Therefore, when I gave assignments verbally, I was annoyed by students who wanted to know the exact number of pages required and whether a paper needed to be double-spaced, typed, or written in blue or black ink. But these students were simply exhibiting their own learning styles and personality types!

Today, in the university courses I teach, my students discover their own learning styles and discuss the implications for their teaching. I encourage them to discover the learning styles of the middle and high school students with whom they work. I strive to use instructional strategies that will engage the variety of learners in my courses and to provide the structure that so many of my students prefer.

### *Questions to Consider*

- To what extent have your educational experiences been appropriate to your personal learning style and individual characteristics?
- What are some of the most memorable learning experiences (good and bad) that you have had in school?

- How will your personal learning style and individual characteristics affect your choice of instructional strategies?

## DIFFERENTIATING INSTRUCTION

Differentiating instruction provides one answer to meeting students' diverse learning needs. It requires modifying instruction to meet students' varying readiness levels, learning preferences, and interests (Lawrence-Brown, 2004; Tomlinson, 2001).

> **CCSSO Principle 3: Adapting Instruction**

Differentiated instruction begins with formal and informal data collection about students' readiness, interest in the content, and learning profile (Brimijoin, Marquissee, & Tomlinson, 2003). Once the teacher has some understanding of who the students are and where they are in their understanding, she can differentiate instruction in three areas: the content, the process, and the product of learning.

*Content* refers to the concepts, principles, and skills that teachers want students to learn. In differentiated instruction, all students learn the same content, but the degree of complexity is adjusted. For example, in a high school biology class, all students learn key understandings about energy and respiration. The teacher, however, provides options for learning the content with different degrees of complexity: some students complete an experiment; some work on study guides; and some use laptop computers to complete a diet planner analyzing how they consume and expend energy in their daily lives (Tomlinson & Doubet, 2005). Providing texts and textbooks at a variety of reading levels is a strategy for differentiating content.

Differentiating *process* refers to the activities student engage in to help them understand and apply the ideas and skills being taught. Strategies such as learning centers, interest groups, mixed-ability groups, journals, learning logs, and concept mapping are a few of the ways to differentiate the processes of learning.

Differentiating *product* refers to culminating projects that allow students to demonstrate and extend what they have learned. The teacher creates criteria for high-quality products and offers students options that will allow them to meet the criteria. For example, students in a Spanish class can demonstrate what they have learned about Mexican culture in a variety of ways: travel guides, documentaries, dramas, or museum exhibits.

Sometimes the teacher may assign students to groups to work on a particular skill, and sometimes students choose their own group. The differentiated classroom capitalizes on diversity: Most students are strong in some areas and weaker in others. Flexible grouping allows all students to extend their strengths and shore up their weaknesses.

## LEARNING IN SMALL GROUPS

Studies have consistently documented the positive effects of small-group learning approaches on the achievement of many different types of students (Slavin, 1995; Slavin & Calderon, 2001). Furthermore, small-group learning arrangements can pro-
mote positive social interactions among students
and enhance positive feelings about self, peers, and
school (Gay, 2002). The problem-solving and social
skills students learn and practice while working in groups are essential for success in the workforce of today and tomorrow (Mandel, 2003).

**CCSSO Principle 2:
Learning and
Human Development**

In small-group learning approaches, students work in groups of four to six to complete a task such as solving algebraic equations, listing pros and cons of protecting endangered species, or constructing an interpretation of a poem. Some group tasks are competitive, such as contests or games that encourage groups to compete against one another. Other group tasks are cooperative, such as working together to apply a formula, prepare a report, or dramatize a scene from literature. Some group tasks are of short duration; others spread over days and weeks (Vermette, 1997).

Small-group learning, however, is not simply a matter of having students
"count off by fours" and "get into groups." Teachers
must consider several factors in order for group work
to succeed (Blumenfeld, Marx, Soloway, & Krajik,
1996).

**CCSSO Principle 5:
Motivation and
Management**

- Establish norms for positive interaction and teach students the skills they need to function successfully as a group.
- Design tasks that lend themselves to group work. A well-designed group task should be complex enough that no single member can complete it satisfactorily. A good task challenges students' thinking and allows for a variety of solutions to a problem.
- Communicate clearly to students the parameters of the task and the criteria for the group product.
- Give students instruction on how to give help effectively (e.g., helping someone arrive at a solution as opposed to giving someone a solution) and how to recognize when and how to ask for help.
- Build in individual accountability through assignment of specific roles and responsibilities to each group member, such as facilita-tor, timekeeper, recorder, and reporter. In addition, students can evaluate their own contributions to the group and the group's success as a whole.

• Consider procedural questions such as:

How will students physically move into groups?
How will the furniture in the classroom be arranged?
How will you distribute and collect materials?
How and when will you give instructions to the groups?

In order to achieve the positive academic and social outcomes mentioned earlier, it makes sense to compose groups that are mixed in ability, ethnicity, and gender (Marzano, Pickering, & Pollock, 2001). Some research, however, suggests that status hierarchies within groups can be detrimental to learning when individuals are viewed by themselves and others as "smart" or "not smart" (Cohen, Kepner, & Swanson, 1995, p. 18).

Jigsaw (Aronson & Patnoe, 1997) is a small-group learning strategy that is appropriate for a wide variety of subjects and grade levels. It is called jigsaw because, like the physical puzzle, each member of a jigsaw group holds a piece of the entire task. For example, in a U.S. history class learning about World War II, the class would be divided into small jigsaw groups of five or six students each. Each member of the jigsaw group is assigned to become an expert on a particular topic, such as concentration camps, Japan's entry into the war, the Normandy invasion, Britain's role in the war, or other relevant topics. Each expert is responsible for learning about that topic through reading an assigned text, whether it be part of a textbook chapter, an informational article, or a website. Next, the jigsaw groups break up into expert groups that consist of all students assigned to the same topic, such as Britain's role in the war. Students in the expert groups help one another to become experts so that each member can go back to her original jigsaw group and teach the others. The time it takes to complete a jigsaw learning activity depends on the amount and difficulty of the content to be learned. Jigsaw is a very efficient way to learn content, but even more important, it makes each student an essential part of the academic learning community and gives everyone experience in collaboration (http://jigsaw.org).

## STUDENT-DIRECTED DISCUSSION

An open discussion is defined as the "free exchange of information among students and/or between at least three participants that lasts longer than 30 seconds" (Applebee, Langer, Nystrand, & Gamoran, 2003, p. 700). Such discussions are characterized by:

**CCSSO Principle 6: Communication Skills**

1. *Authentic questions* designed to explore differing understandings rather than to "test what students might

already know"; 2. *Teacher "uptake,"* in which a teacher's question takes up and builds on a student's previous comment, creating continuity in the discussion (Applebee et al., p. 690). Participants in open discussions ask questions primarily for purposes of clarification, as they take positions, express opinions, and explore personal reactions. Such purposeful talk helps students develop higher-order thinking skills.

The *Socratic seminar* takes its name from the Greek philosopher Socrates, who was noted for his style of teaching by asking probing questions, thus encouraging *divergent* rather than *convergent* thinking in his students. This method of student-directed discussion requires students to read, think, and respond critically. It also teaches students skills in speaking, listening, values clarification, and conflict resolution (Adler, 1982; Polite & Adams, 1997). It is appropriate in any content area and meets the goals of interdisciplinary teaching (Tanner & Casados, 1998).

The teacher's role is to ask clarifying questions, paraphrase ideas, and help students move ahead if they get stuck in their discussion. The teacher models appropriate behavior–respectful listening, courteous interaction, and thinking. Experienced seminar leaders report that at first they fear loss of control, but as teacher and students become more comfortable with the method, teachers report how much they enjoy "the renewed spirit and authentic experience of being in a learning community" (Tredway, 1995, p. 28).

Students prepare for a Socratic seminar by reading a common text and writing questions to bring to the table. Seats are often arranged in an inner and outer circle. Students who sit in the inner circle actively participate in the discussion. Students who sit in the outer circle take notes, summarize, and reflect on the discussion. At least one seat is left open in the inner circle, which may be taken by any person seated in the outer circle who wants to get into the discussion. Seminars last from 30 to 80 minutes, but should be wrapped up when the discussion seems to be running out of steam. A debriefing follows the seminar, during which students in the outer circle present their analyses and observations of the process and content of the seminar.

## STUDENTS TEACHING STUDENTS

Most teachers know that teaching something to someone is one of the best ways to learn it. With guidance, students can be effective teachers of other students. In this section, two strategies for students teaching students are presented.

## Reciprocal Teaching

*Reciprocal teaching* is a structured form of peer tutoring that emphasizes reading comprehension, the source of many students' academic difficulties (Carter, 1997). The strategy is especially appropriate to reading expository material, such as subject area textbooks. The general approach is to have students read a passage of material, paragraph by paragraph, aloud to a partner or small group. The teacher needs to model the process of reading and questioning when introducing the strategy. During the reading, students learn and practice four essential comprehension strategies:

- generating questions
- summarizing
- clarifying word meanings or confusing text
- predicting what might appear in the next paragraph
  (Rosenshine & Meister, 1994)

The partner or other students in the group participate by elaborating or commenting on the reader's summary, suggesting other questions, commenting on predictions, requesting additional clarification, and helping to resolve misunderstandings.

Reciprocal teaching provides practice in using strategies to read real text, not fabricated exercises. It provides support for students as they develop reading strategies. Finally, students support other students in developing these strategies (Rosenshine & Meister, 1994).

## Peer Tutoring

Some students need a lot more help than others in mastering the content or skills being taught. Peer tutoring can be an effective way to provide that extra help (Walberg & Paik, 2004). Within the classroom, you might set up peer study groups in which higher-achieving students help lower-achieving students apply skills or concepts you have introduced. For such an arrangement to be successful, however, you must be sensitive to the needs of both the tutors (who may feel they are being used) and the tutees (who may feel stigmatized).

Some peer-tutoring advocates propose randomly assigning pairs who alternate roles of tutor and tutee. In this arrangement (classwide peer tutoring), everyone gets the chance to learn and to teach. Classwide peer tutoring is especially effective in inclusive classrooms, benefiting both general and special education students academically and socially (King-Sears & Cummings, 1996).

Cross-age tutoring is more challenging to arrange but may be more beneficial to both tutors and tutees. For example, eighth graders who are having difficulty with reading can be trained to help younger students (e.g., fourth or sixth graders) who are also having difficulty with reading. Studies have shown that cross-age tutoring benefits both parties, particularly when low achievers assume the role of tutor (Friedland & Truesdell, 2006; Paterson & Elliott, 2006).

## THINKING SKILLS REVISITED

Deductive teaching, described in Chapter 8, is closely associated with teacher-directed instructional strategies. *Inductive teaching* might be viewed as a more student-centered strategy. Inductive thinking is "the process of drawing new conclusions based on information we know or are presented with" (Marzano, Pickering, & Pollack, 2001, p. 104). A teacher who takes a deductive approach, for example, might ask students to watch Olympic events on television and classify sports into predetermined categories. A teacher who takes an inductive approach asks students to generate their own categories for the events they view (Marzano et al., 2001).

### Theory into Practice

Below is a reflective vignette written by Nick Sevano, who teaches English in a large, urban high school. As you read, think about what you have read about helping students develop thinking and reasoning skills, then answer the questions that follow.

### *That Horrible Freedom:*
### *An Inductive Approach to High School Composition*

"So you want us to do what?"

It's never verbalized; no one raises even a tentative hand to express the confusion felt in the room. Attempting to morph their frustration into a teachable moment, I tell each student in my 10th grade English class to look around the room at their peers and then write down a short description of what they see on one another's faces. I emphasize that they should write down what they see and not how they see it. Now it's time to go around the room in ninety seconds:

"Jenni was staring at the floor."

"Natasha's mouth was open."

"Christopher's eyebrows were raised."

I then lead them into a short discussion about what these observations suggest, exemplify, or reveal. And for the second time that period, I introduce the inductive approach to writing about literature.

Not until I became a college student did I realize that academic writing was not something to which I had been exposed in high school. In college, there was no one present to guide the writing process, to question the validity of my arguments, or to offer helpful suggestions. For the entire process, I was on my own. That horrible freedom revealed that writing an academic paper was a slippery inductive process.

A deductive approach to teaching writing is safe: the teacher identifies a topic, such as symbolism, in a piece of literature. The students search the text for examples of symbolism as defined by the teacher, and ultimately write an essay with a thesis provided by the teacher. The deductive movement establishes a safe paradigm for students: they write, for the most part, without the threat of uncertainty.

An inductive approach to composition removes the intellectual safety net. In an inductive approach, students reason from particular experiences to general truths. They forge connections between and among details, words, images, structural devices; they construct arguments as they decode and unpack language; they judge the validity of their assertions, discovering how arguments shift and evolve.

As an introduction to induction, I had my students go on an independent field trip to Starbucks. They were to order a drink, sit in the cafe, and observe everything. I explained that every item in the cafe—from object placement to graphic representation—was a result of careful and deliberate calculation. Students were to identify as many details as possible, classify each detail on the sheet I provided and draw conclusions based on those details.

Students then wrote up a report of their observations focused on a thesis derived from their observations, such as "Starbucks is committed to greening the environment" or "Starbucks is designed to appeal to pseudo-intellectual liberals." We then applied the same process to analyzing literary texts. I am still experimenting with ways to teach writing inductively, but I feel that I am now doing a better job equipping my students not only for academic writing but for life. After all, as my colleague Sherwin reminds me often, "Everything is an example of something."

***Questions to Consider.*** Nick's vignette provides a good example of how teachers use reflection to implement standards-based teaching. Nick reflected on his own experience as a student and on the experiences of his current students (who were probably all familiar with Starbucks) to teach them an inductive approach to writing literary analysis, a skill which is commonly included in standards for high school English. Without reflection, Nick might have stuck to the tried-and-true deductive assignment he described above and his students might have produced proficient but predictable literary essays. Instead, he designed an approach that taught students to find their own topics and themes and helped them become independent learners and thinkers.

- How do you react to Nick's claim that his high school learning experiences did not prepare him for the "horrible freedom" of college learning?
- How could you use induction in your own subject area?
- Do you agree with Nick's claim that by teaching his students induction he is doing a better job preparing them for life?

## TEACHING FOR UNDERSTANDING

When teachers feel pressured to cover content, depth of understanding may be sacrificed. Students who learn at different paces and in different styles

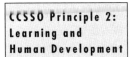

are often left behind, and those who do keep up may lack true understanding: "the capacity to take knowledge learned in one setting and apply it appropriately in a different setting" (Gardner, quoted in Brandt, 1993, p. 4). The strategies presented in this section give students the opportunity to develop depth of knowledge by giving them some control over the pace, content, mode, and processes of learning (Rief, 1996).

### Learning Centers

Teachers use learning centers to tailor instruction to student needs and interests, to give students choice and responsibility for their own learning, and to offer meaningful learning experiences to students who are working at different paces. A learning center is usually a physical space in the classroom where individuals or small groups can work independently on activities.

Learning centers can be organized in a number of different ways. A foreign language teacher, for example, might maintain learning centers at which students can study and acquire vocabulary through their preferred learning style. A middle school science teacher might teach photosynthesis by having students read about the concept (linguistic), use diagrams or pictures (spatial), analyze the sequence of the process (logical-mathematical), dramatize the process (bodily-kinesthetic), create a song about it (musical), work in groups (interpersonal), and do a reflective activity, such as comparing photosynthesis to a change in their own lives (intrapersonal). Learning centers can also be organized thematically. For example, if a social studies class is studying Africa, learning centers might offer students the chance to explore areas of interest such as music, art, literature, food, youth culture, or entertainment (Tiedt & Tiedt, 2001).

## Learning Activity Packets

Learning activity packets are self-guided units of instruction or activities that students can work through with minimal teacher guidance. They can be used as enrichment for students who complete required assignments early or as review and reinforcement for students who need extra practice. They can even be used as the foundation for entire self-directed units of study (Tiedt & Tiedt, 2001). Packets should include whole-class activities as well as provisions for individual work on vocabulary, reading comprehension, and writing skills. With packets, students can progress at their own pace and can easily catch up following absences (Smith & Manley, 1994).

## Learning Contracts

Learning contracts are written agreements between students and teachers that give students some flexibility and choice in what they will study and how they will demonstrate learning. At the same time, the contract provides clear expectations for performance and criteria for success. Contracts can be effective for giving students both freedom and responsibility and can be useful in a variety of situations. You can negotiate contracts with students who will be absent for extended periods. Sometimes staffing and enrollment issues necessitate teaching classes with more than one level of student. Learning contracts can be drawn up for independent study or experiential learning that enriches the classroom curriculum.

Learning contracts allow students to make choices about the content, pace, and structure of their learning. Some allow students to select the grade they wish to receive and clearly state the criteria students must meet to receive that grade. When the parameters of the project and performance criteria are clearly stated, learning contracts can be effective and offer another way to differentiate instruction (Greenwood & McCabe, 2008; Willems, McConnell, & Willems, 1997).

## LITERACY IN THE CONTENT AREAS

Increasingly, students arrive at middle and high school unable to read academic text fluently. Some struggle with reading academic texts because they are still learning English; others have never acquired the skills of fluent readers, and many have grown quite adept at concealing that fact (Scala, 2001). As they progress in school, students need to learn reading strategies more sophisticated than those they learned in fourth grade. Middle and high school readers should be able to:

- Question themselves about what they read;
- Synthesize information from various sources;
- Identify, understand, and remember key vocabulary;
- Recognize how a text is organized and use that organization as a tool for learning;
- Organize information in notes;
- Interpret diverse symbol systems in subjects such as biology and algebra;
- Search the Internet for information;
- Judge their own understanding;
- Evaluate authors' ideas and perspectives (Moore, Bean, Birdyshaw, & Rycik, 1999)

Recently, the National Commission on Writing in America's Schools and Colleges (2003) stated:

> If students are to make knowledge their own, they must struggle with the details, wrestle with the facts, and rework raw information and dimly understood concepts into language they can communicate to someone else. In short, if students are to learn, they must write. (p. 9)

Many teachers use learning logs, journals, or diaries to encourage students to record their understandings of the content (Murray, 2001). For example, a physics teacher might have students keep "inquiry diaries" in which they connect physics concepts to personal experience (Tishman, Perkins, & Jay, 1994).

*Admit slips* are brief written responses that are turned in to the teacher at the beginning of class. An admit slip might request a personal response to a reading assignment, a homework problem, or a question for discussion. The teacher collects the slips as students enter the room and uses them to determine what concepts and vocabulary she needs to introduce and review.

*Exit slips* are completed and turned in to the teacher at the end of class. An exit slip might require students to summarize what they have learned that day, write down questions they still have, or evaluate the day's activities. Both admit and exit slips help students learn in greater depth while giving the teacher important information about their ongoing progress (Gere, 1985).

Writing to learn can take many other forms. For example, math students can write their own problems or write explanations of problem-solving strategies for an audience of younger students. Science students can sketch the night sky and record their reactions to its beauty in poetry or prose. History students can write obituaries of important figures.

## MAKING CONNECTIONS
## TO THE WORLD BEYOND THE CLASSROOM

Good teachers create pedagogical bridges that help students connect prior knowledge with new knowledge and abstract knowledge with lived experience (Gay, 2002). Strategies such as role-playing, simulations, and drama help students make connections between content and their own lives. Problem-based learning approaches can extend beyond classroom walls and into the community.

### Drama in the Classroom

Role-playing, simulation, and drama offer students the opportunity to personally connect with content; to improve their interpersonal, presentational, and reflective skills; and to develop a better understanding of multiple perspectives on issues. Furthermore, students gain experience in problem solving and decision making (Joyce, Weil, & Calhoun, 2004). A classroom climate of trust and respect is essential if students are to benefit from participating in dramatizations.

> **CCSSO Principle 6:**
> **Communication Skills**

*Role-play.* Role-play enables participants to put themselves in the shoes of another person and to rehearse behavior with some reality and in a safe environment for trying out new ideas. Role-plays may be used to address social issues, interpersonal conflicts, intergroup relations, individual dilemmas, and historical or contemporary problems. For role-plays to be successful, students must act out their roles with believability and the roles or situation must have a real-life quality. It is important that debriefing and evaluating occur after enactment (Joyce, Weil, & Calhoun, 2004).

***Simulations.*** Simulations may require students to assume roles for extended periods of time or to do research in preparation for their task or role. Simulations are generally more structured than role-plays and the outcomes more predictable. For example, students might enact the roles of a space flight crew facing an emergency, act as advisors to the United States government, or learn the rules and assume the roles of a different culture. Simulations may be teacher-developed, but are also commercially available. Technology, too, is helping to create ever more sophisticated simulations. For example, StockQuest (http://investsmart.coe.uga.edu/C001759) helps students learn about investing by giving them 100,000 fantasy dollars to invest in stocks.

***Dramatic Activities.*** Dramatic activities provide opportunities for students to make connections to the world beyond the classroom (Heathcote & Bolton, 1994). Dramatic techniques are especially engaging for students who learn best through movement and physical involvement. Students can dramatize texts in print or write and enact their own stories. They can form tableaux, or still lifes, of critical moments in a literary text, a historical event, or a chemical reaction. Pantomime can be used to show scientific, economic, legal, or interpersonal processes. Students can write, rehearse, direct, and produce skits and plays in all subjects.

## Problem-Based Learning

In problem-based learning approaches, students are presented with a genuine problem, puzzle, or mystery. Minimal time is spent on lecture, and the teacher acts primarily as a resource and facilitator. Students serve as resources for one another and perform their work both independently and in small groups. Following are guidelines for planning a problem-based learning experience:

| CCSSO Principle 2: |
| Learning and |
| Human Development |

- Begin with a problem that connects with the students' world.
- Organize subject matter around the problem, not around the disciplines.
- Give students major responsibility for shaping and directing their own learning.
- Use small teams as the context for most learning.
- Require students to demonstrate what they have learned through a product or performance (Savoie & Hughes, 1994).

Problem-based learning is democratic because students work together toward a common goal. The solution of complex problems requires everyone, regardless of ability or disability, to contribute. Students are motivated to engage in it because it is authentic and contextualized, allows them to interact with a variety of individuals, and involves them in processes that give them ownership of the projects (Slavkin, 2004).

## SUMMARY

The strategies presented in this chapter and the preceding one can help foster authentic intellectual achievement. These strategies met four standards for authentic pedagogy:

1. encouraging higher-order thinking
2. holding substantive conversations
3. developing depth of knowledge
4. connecting to the world beyond the classroom

You should use these standards to monitor the quality of the instructional strategies you choose.

The strategies introduced in this chapter were characterized as *student-centered*, but this was primarily an organizational device: All good teaching strategies require teacher direction and should be appropriate to student needs and characteristics. Among the key points to remember are:

- Differentiating instruction means modifying content, processes, and products to meet students' varying readiness levels, learning preferences, and interests.
- Cooperative learning approaches, like jigsaw, can promote academic achievement, positive social interactions among students, and positive feelings about self, peers, and school.
- Open discussion and Socratic seminars provide alternatives to the teacher-initiate/student-respond pattern of classroom discussion.
- Students can often be effective teachers of other students.
- Learning centers, activity packets, and contracts provide ways to deepen understanding and differentiate instruction.
- Today, all teachers should know some strategies for teaching reading and writing to learn.
- Drama- and problem-based learning approaches can help students connect content to their own experiences and to the world beyond the classroom.

## *Reflecting on the Standards*

- How could you use any of the strategies described in this chapter to adapt instruction to student responses, ideas, and needs?
- What are your personal characteristics that might predispose you to implement some strategies described in this chapter and not others?
- Which strategies seem most likely to foster students' critical thinking and independent problem solving?
- How could you use one or more of these strategies to enhance learning in your subject area?

# CHAPTER 10

# Assessing Student Learning

One of the greatest challenges teachers face is determining how to collect, interpret, record, and report evidence of student learning in equitable, defensible, and understandable ways. In addition, teachers are challenged to administer and interpret the results of a variety of standardized tests. Ultimately, your job is to use the information gathered from assessment and evaluation to help students judge their success in learning and to help you improve instruction.

The overall purpose of this chapter is related to CCSSO Principle #8: *The teacher understands and uses formal and informal assessment strategies to evaluate and ensure the continuous intellectual, social, and physical development of the learner.*

Specifically, this chapter will help you:

- Become familiar with some key terms in assessment;
- Understand the characteristics, uses, advantages, and limitations of various types of assessments;
- Design appropriate assessments of student learning;
- Develop strategies to involve learners in self-assessment;
- Consider issues involved in assigning and reporting grades;
- Understand the role of standardized tests in monitoring student learning.

### REFLECTING ON PRACTICE: LIZ SPALDING– "FROM POINT COLLECTOR TO THOUGHTFUL ASSESSOR"

As a student, I was generally a good test-taker: I could usually figure out what the teacher thought was important and remember it long enough to fill in the blanks, choose the right answer, or match terms to definitions. Essay tests were not a problem, since I was a fluent writer. My test-taking prowess enabled me to earn high grades in most of my school subjects. High grades affirmed that I was good at certain subjects, such as English and foreign languages. My low grades in math and science proved I wasn't good at those subjects. Consequently, I did not enjoy these classes, nor did I work hard in them.

When I began teaching, I found myself in the position of test-maker rather than test-taker. As a test-maker, I was guided by my own experiences as a student, what other teachers around me were doing, by what students seemed to expect, and by prepackaged tests that accompanied the textbooks I used. For example, in my English classes, I would assign spelling or vocabulary words on Monday for a quiz on Friday. On Tuesday, I would assign a short story to be read as homework. On Wednesday, I would give a quiz to determine whether students had read and understood the story. Eventually I would give a test covering the spelling, vocabulary, and stories. This routine enabled me to sit down with a calculator at the end of each 9 weeks, compute the number of points possible, and determine what percentage of this number each student had earned. I allotted some number of points for participation, so that I could reward students for their effort or progress (and penalize students who were lazy or disruptive). I didn't use this information in order to make instructional decisions or analyze student learning. I was primarily a point collector.

Over the years, my assessment practices improved. I developed more systematic ways to assign value to student work so that one low test score, for example, would not have a devastating impact on a student's overall grade. I devised projects that allowed students to demonstrate their understanding in ways other than paper-and-pencil tests. I recorded students' contributions to class discussions as evidence of their class participation. Whenever possible, I offered students opportunities to revise their work before submitting it for a grade. Nevertheless, grading remained a painful issue for me. I still struggle with designing assessments that fairly reflect what students know and can do, that make criteria for success clear to all, and that encourage students to become thoughtful assessors of their own performance.

### Questions to Consider

- What kind of test-taker are you?
- Do you recall a particularly good experience with testing? A particularly bad experience? What did you learn from that experience?
- How might your own experience with tests influence how you test as a teacher?

# UNDERSTANDING THE LANGUAGE OF ASSESSMENT

As a classroom teacher you will be continuously conducting *assessment*: the process of gathering information in a valid, timely, and efficient manner in order to make decisions about teaching and learning. *Formative assessment* is the process of gathering information while work is still in progress in order to influence the final outcome. *Summative assessment* or *evaluation* is the process of using and interpreting the information collected during the formative stage to make decisions (National Center for Fair and Open Testing, 2006). In the classroom, this usually translates into a unit test or a significant product or performance that demonstrates what the student has learned. A grade assigned at the end of a 9-week grading period, semester, or course also represents summative assessment.

In school, as students are working toward a goal, they need lots of feedback (formative assessment) along the way to help them achieve a desired outcome. Once their work is evaluated (summative assessment), they need feedback that will help them progress toward the next learning goal. Teachers should use the information gained from formative and summative assessment to make decisions about what students still need to learn and how they might go about learning it.

Good assessments are both valid and reliable. A *valid test* accurately assesses the skills or knowledge in question. Determining how many square feet of carpet are needed to remodel a room is a highly valid test of measuring skill. A *reliable test* consistently measures what it claims to measure. On the one hand, a multiple-choice test on measurement might be extremely reliable— that is, it could be administered year after year to many different groups of test takers with fairly predictable results. In addition, it can be scored reliably because all questions have one right answer. On the other hand, actually measuring a bedroom may be an extremely valid test, but it may not always be reliable: one student might use a ruler to measure; another might use a cloth tape measure; another might use a carpenter's retractable measure.

Most large-scale, standardized testing is *norm-referenced*. That is, it is based on the assumption that a few will excel, a few will fail, but most will perform in the middle range (i.e., the norm) (National Center for Fair and Open Testing, 2006). Norm-referenced tests compare students to one another, so scores are reported in relation to the performance of the whole group. For example, a score in the 93rd *percentile* means that the test-taker has performed better than 93% of people taking the test and not as well as the 7% who scored better. In addition, scores are often reported as *grade-equivalent scores* (GES). A grade equivalent score indicates the grade and month of the school year for which a score is average. For example, the average score of a seventh grader being tested in the seventh month of the school year would be 7.7. If a seventh grader receives a GES of 10.1 on a reading comprehension test, that means she or he has scored the same as an average entering tenth grader taking the test (Mertler, 2004).

Some large-scale tests are *criterion-referenced*: a standard of mastery is set and everyone works toward that standard. State and district proficiency exams are generally criterion-referenced, since the goal is for everyone to meet the criteria (or standards) for proficiency.

## MINIMIZING BIAS AND INCREASING EQUITY

*Bias* in assessment is the extent to which the task advantages or disadvantages the test-taker. Bias can arise because of geographical, socioeconomic, religious, cultural, and linguistic differences. Often, bias in testing is rooted in the assumption that all students have access to the same knowledge as that possessed by White, middle-class Americans. Students today have widely differing backgrounds, experiences, and access to resources. These differences must be taken into account when tests—especially high-stakes tests—are designed. A great deal of evidence points to the fact that assessment and evaluation practices in this country—from the classroom quiz to large-scale standardized tests of achievement or IQ—have been unfair to a large number of students, especially those with linguistic, cultural, and ethnic differences, students with disabilities, and those from low-income families (Farr & Trumbull, 1997; Hanson, 1993; Hilliard, 1990).

| CCSSO Principle 3: Adopting Instruction |
|---|

*Equity* in assessment means giving all students opportunities to demonstrate what they actually know in a given subject area. English Language Learners may know a great deal about the subject in question but cannot yet fluently express what they know in English. Students with reading difficulties may not be able to demonstrate what they know under the same time limits imposed on those who read quickly. Test items that rely on cultural knowledge, such as computing a bill in a restaurant or planning a skiing vacation, may disadvantage students who have never eaten in a restaurant or vacationed anywhere at all. Students with disabilities need the same accommodations during assessments as they receive during instruction, such as listening to material on tape or making use of a scribe (Shriner, Ysseldyke, Thurlow, & Honetschlager, 1994).

## ASSESSMENT AND EVALUATION IN THE CLASSROOM

Teachers gather information about student performance from a variety of sources for a variety of purposes and audiences. At the beginning of the school year, many teachers gather information from students and use it to plan for instruction while getting to know their students. Surveys of students' interests and attitudes provide information that can help teachers plan instruction and assessments as well as monitor student engagement with learning. Observation can reveal a great deal about what students are learning (or not learning). Interviews and conferences can also be valuable sources of information about student learning (Hill & Ruptic, 1994; Paris & Ayres, 1994).

## Theory into Practice: Preparing for State Testing

Victoria Majeski (a pseudonym) wrote the following reflection during her semester as a long-term substitute teacher in the English Department of a high school in a medium-sized city in the Southeast. Historically, the high school has not performed well on the state's high-stakes accountability tests, so Victoria was very conscious of her responsibility to prepare students to do well.

> **CCSSO Principle 7:**
> **Planning**

When I accepted a long-term sub position in the English Department, I knew that building vocabulary was essential to enable my students to read more effectively. Increasing vocabulary was especially important for my sophomores, who were gearing up to take their ACT/SATs and to participate in state testing. So, one day after a very long faculty meeting during which we discussed how to prepare our students for state testing, I decided that it was time to revamp my approach to reviewing vocabulary, a task my students had come to dread.

Late that night, I decided to create a vocabulary quiz game. While quickly writing questions such as "Define 'jargon'" or "True or False: a wing nut is 'edible'," I realized that answering eighty questions about word meaning could get boring (and if you're the teacher and are bored, there is no hope that the students will be entertained). So, I decided to intersperse two different types of questions unrelated to the vocabulary. I used "Name that Tune" questions to keep the competition friendly, connect with the students, and to simply make the game more fun (In fact, I was so excited making the questions, I had little doubt that the students would enjoy them). I made a music CD including songs popular when I was in high school and songs currently popular with my students. The second type of question was related to events and people at the school. These questions were designed to boost student morale and recognize accomplishment.

The next day, I introduced the game to each of my classes. After teams were formed and named, each team received a clacker as a means for ringing in to answer (another avenue for making the game fun and light-hearted). Teams were allowed to use class notes, which fostered teamwork because each student became personally responsible for a certain number of vocabulary packets and answering questions. As a prize, the highest scoring team would receive ten extra credit points applied to their participation grade.

After several rounds of vocabulary items, I came to the first "Name That Tune" question. The first song was "Jump" by Kris Kross. Students recognized it and erupted into excitement, jumping out of their seats to answer the question. That day, students who had never participated before were actively answering questions. One young man answered more questions than any other student– he had never spoken a word to me before that game.

Even after the administration of the state tests, we continued to play the game periodically. As a result, students more readily completed their homework packets and their in-class test scores came up significantly. We have not yet received our score reports from the state tests, but I am hoping to see improved reading scores.

When planning it, I wasn't sure this game would work. To me, it felt like a shoddy attempt to disguise reviewing vocabulary. To the students, however, it was an outlet because it combined fun and school, review and music. Test preparation doesn't have to be drudgery. I needed to prepare my students for the state test and they needed to let loose, since they had been reviewing information in all classes to prepare for testing. I think we accomplished both.

### Questions to Consider

- What are the strengths and potential weaknesses of Victoria's approach to vocabulary assessment?
- How does this vignette show what Victoria understands about formal and informal assessment and about students' social, intellectual, and physical development?

## Planning "Backwards" for Assessment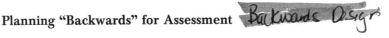

Identifying the outcomes or targets of instruction should be the first step in planning for assessment (Wiggins & McTighe, 2005). This holds true for planning a course, a semester, a unit, or a lesson. Once you have identified the target, you can then plan "backwards" to ensure that students learn the skills that will enable them to reach your goals.

One example of planning backwards to design a course comes from a team of math and science teachers at Central Park East Secondary School in New York City (Meier, 2002). The team decided to focus their curriculum on the big ideas of forces, motion, and the conservation of energy. They designed a final assessment in which students would use what they knew about these ideas to design scary but safe amusement park rides. They then identified the knowledge and skills students would need to be successful in the culminating task and planned the curriculum backwards to include such concepts as mass, volume, and velocity and such skills as computing area vs. volume, solving linear vs. nonlinear equations, probability, trigonometry, and basic arithmetic skills. Formulating the final assessment in advance enabled the teachers to be more focused in their instruction and the students to be aware of the expectations for learning.

## Assigning Value to Habits We Value

Often the behaviors and habits of mind we value most in students—inquisitiveness, persistence, attention to detail, the asking of important questions, and a willingness to help others—are inadequately reflected in the assessments they complete and the grades they are assigned (Wiggins, 1993). It is just as important to assess the processes of learning as the products.

It is possible to design defensible and fair ways to assess the processes of learning. For example, in designing group projects, many teachers have developed techniques to assess group process as well as final product, and they require students to submit written reflections concerning their contributions to the group and the group's success as a team.

Learning logs and journals are additional sources of information about whether students are developing habits of mind we value and deepening their understanding of subject matter. Students can use these tools to summarize their understanding of the day's material, express how they feel about it, respond to a subject-related prompt, record research activities, take notes, and jot down sources that remain to be consulted (Murray, 2001).

## Helping Students Become Self-Assessors

We know that successful people—athletes, actors and actresses, trial lawyers, and surgeons, for example—constantly monitor their own performance and modify what they do on the basis of this information (Gladwell, 1999). What can teachers do to help students become skilled self-assessors and independent and lifelong learners?

Techniques such as learning logs, conferences, and reflections on group process promote student self-assessment. Because most students are not accustomed to assessing their own performance, their first attempts at self-assessment may be disappointingly vague or brief. You may need to provide students with scaffolding—prompts and structured questionnaires to help them complete an unfamiliar task. These can gradually be removed as students develop skills in reflection and see that their opinions are valued.

## TRADITIONAL FORMS OF CLASSROOM ASSESSMENT

As a student yourself for so many years, you have undoubtedly experienced many of the traditional forms of classroom assessment, from reading comprehension quizzes to short answer and long essay tests. All these forms have value when they are used to provide you and your students with feedback on learning.

### Objective Test Items

Objective quizzes and tests—those containing items that are designed to have only one correct answer—are an efficient way to gather information. Many textbooks come with prepackaged tests and quizzes, as well as item banks from which you can construct your own customized tests. Like microwaveable frozen dinners, these ready-made tools can make your life easier but should be used judiciously.

Research suggests that traditional, teacher-made, objective tests generally call for knowledge of facts, even when teachers claim to value higher-order thinking (Madaus & Kellaghan, 1996). Table 10.1 presents guidelines for constructing common types of traditional test items.

### Essay Questions

Well-written essay questions are more likely than objective items to elicit higher-order thinking such as analysis, synthesis, and evaluation. An essay question that simply requires students to recall facts, however (e.g., "List the life stages of a cell and explain the function of each"), does not serve the purpose of essay items. A well-written essay item:

- Clearly states the expectations for the response;
- Suggests time to be spent on and point value of each question or portion of the question;
- Gives students as much information as possible about the requirements of a full response.

**TABLE 10.1. Guidelines for Constructing Objective Test Items**

| Multiple-Choice | True/False | Matching | Fill-in-the Blank |
|---|---|---|---|
| Structure the stem and choices so that they are succinct. | Use precise language. | Construct homogeneous categories for matching. For example, don't mix dates, people, and events in one set of items. | The desired response should be definite and brief. |
| Avoid repetition of phrases and terms. | Avoid indefinite terms such as *more, few, large.* | | Make all response blanks of equal length. |
| | Be sure the statement is entirely true or entirely false. | Keep the list of matching items brief (5–10). | Avoid grammatical clues, such as *is/are* or *she/he* preceding the blank. |
| Minimize use of negative terms (*no, none, never*) and absolutes (*always, all, very*). | Challenge students but do not "trick" them. | Include a few distracters that don't match any items. | Avoid excessive use of blanks within one question. |
| Limit the use of *all of the above* and *none of the above* as choices. | Instruct students to write out the words *true* or *false* to avoid confusion between *t* and *f* when scoring. | Specify whether an item can be used more than once in your directions. | Make sure the item includes sufficient context to elicit the desired response. |
| Proofread to ensure that only one correct answer is offered for each item. | Consider asking students to correct false statements; this discourages guessing. | Work through the items yourself to check for feasibility. | Regardless of where the blank appears in the item, consider having students write responses in blanks in the left margin; this requires less eye movement when you are grading. |
| Proofread for grammatical correctness. | | | |
| Work through the items yourself to check for feasibility. | Work through the items yourself to check for feasibility. | | Complete the items yourself to check for feasibility. |

Encourage students to spend some time planning before they begin writing. Because essays are written under time constraints, it is not advisable to hold students accountable for written mechanics. One excellent way to determine the feasibility of an essay question is to write out the answer yourself in advance.

### Teaching Study and Test-Taking Skills

Many students perform poorly on tests because they lack study skills and knowledge of test-taking strategies. Because many tests require recall of information, you can teach students strategies for remembering facts, such as repetition, visualization, rhymes, graphic organizers, abbreviations, and acronymic sentences (Strichart, Mangrum & Iannuzzi, 2001).

| CCSSO Principle 3: Adapting Instruction |
|---|

You can help students prepare for tests by presenting a plan for studying and by teaching test-taking skills. For example, you can teach an overall strategy for approaching a test, such as DETER. DETER is an acronym for a five-step approach to test-taking. The letters stand for 1. read the *Directions*; 2. *Examine* the entire test to see what is required; 3. decide how much *Time* to allot to items and parts; 4. begin with the *Easiest* parts; 5. *Review* your answers when you have finished.

## ALTERNATIVE FORMS
## OF CLASSROOM ASSESSMENT

Teachers in some subjects have been doing performance assessment for years. When students drive in a driver education course or carry on a conversation in a foreign language class, they are demonstrating their mastery by performing. Performance assessment helps students make connections between school knowledge and real-life knowledge. Because performance assessment is intended to replicate real-world applications of knowledge, it is also referred to as *authentic* assessment.

In designing performance assessment tasks, you must attend to at least three critical features:

- the task must be linked to meaningful learner outcomes and students must see these links;
- the task must be clearly structured so that all students can understand what is expected of them;
- students should be well aware of the criteria by which their response will be scored.

## FIGURE 10.1. Performance Task Formats

| | | |
|---|---|---|
| Autobiography | Friendly letter | Pamphlet |
| Blog | Game | Parody |
| Book chapter | Grant application | Photo essay |
| Bulletin board | Graph | Poster |
| Business letter | Interview | PowerPoint® |
| Cartoon or comic | Journal |    presentation |
| Children's book | Lab report | Research report |
| Composing a song | Land use survey | Science fair display |
| Data table | Letter asking | Scrap book |
| Digital story |    for information | Skit |
| Display | Letter to the editor | Survey |
| Drawing | Management plan | Travel brochure |
| Editorial | Map | Tribute or eulogy |
| Ethnic food | Model | Video |
| Experiment | Monologue | Weather map |
| Expository essay | Movie | Web site |
| Fairy tale | Observation | Wiki |
| Folk tale | Oral report | |

Figure 10.1 contains examples of products that students could create to demonstrate their learning in various subject areas.

## Using Rubrics to Score Performance

If you've ever used a AAA® or Michelin guide to lodgings and restaurants, you have seen a *rubric*: a set of clear, concise statements that detail the qualities that distinguish among poor, fair, good, and outstanding establishments. *Analytic rubrics* are used to assign scores along several major dimensions of the performance. Students receive scores for such categories as collaboration, aesthetics, or English usage. Points earned in each category are added to achieve a total score. *Holistic rubrics* assign a single score to a performance. In the classroom, analytic rubrics provide more feedback to students than holistic rubrics, but assigning a holistic score is less time-consuming. The choice of rubrics depends on the purpose and audience of the assessment.

Goodrich (1996/1997) has recommended the following guidelines for developing and using rubrics with students:

1. Look at models. Show students examples of good and poor work and discuss the qualities that distinguish a good performance from a poor one.
2. List criteria. Use the discussion to generate a list of the distinguishing features of quality work.

3. Describe gradations of quality. Describe the top and the bottom levels first, then fill in the middle levels.
4. Practice on models. Have students practice applying the rubric to the models used in Step One.
5. Use peer- and self-assessment. As students work on a task, have them periodically apply the rubric to their emerging work or have it assessed by a peer.
6. Revise. Students should revise based on the information gained in Step Five.
7. Use the same rubric students used when you assess their work. (pp. 16–17)

When teachers in a department or school collaborate on developing tasks, rubrics, and exemplars, then scoring becomes a form of professional development. The conversations teachers have about what constitutes a task worth doing, what distinguishes quality work from work that is mediocre, and how one knows quality work when one sees it can lead to important insights about improving teaching and learning (Allen, 1998; Stiggins, 2004).

## Portfolios

*Portfolios*, collections of student work produced over some period of time, have become a widely used tool for assessment. Models, artists, architects, and others have long used portfolios to demonstrate what they know and can do. Portfolio keepers regularly select from the whole body of their work and arrange selections to fit a particular purpose. In the classroom, students can use portfolios to show different facets of themselves as learners.

Some of the benefits of using portfolios for classroom assessment include:

- Portfolios offer "the opportunity to observe students in a broader context: taking risks, developing creative solutions, and learning to make judgments about their own performances."
- Portfolios allow a student to be "a participant in, rather than the object of, assessment."
- Portfolios encourage "students to develop the abilities needed to become independent, self-directed learners" (Paulson, Paulson, & Meyer, 1991, p. 63).

In the classroom, students collect their work in folders. Periodically, they select work from their folders to be revised or polished for inclusion in their portfolios. Students regularly reflect on the work completed or in progress and, ultimately, on the whole body of work in the portfolio in order to assess their own learning, accomplishments, strengths, and weaknesses, and to set future goals (Paulson & Paulson, 1992).

Helping students to reflect on their work is probably the greatest challenge of portfolio assessment, but it is crucial to achieving its benefits. Reflection is the process of looking back on a learning experience and articulating what one has learned from it (Camp, 1992; Paris & Ayres, 1994).

Paulson and Paulson (1992) have described a "continuum of reflectivity" along which students move as they practice reflection: 1. "What I did"–the ability to state what is contained in the portfolio; 2. "What I learned"–the ability to make claims to specific learnings and to substantiate those claims by making reference to changing behaviors, attitudes, and practices; and 3. "What's next"–the ability to formulate, implement, and monitor "necessary next steps for professional and personal growth" (pp. 12–13).

The role the portfolio plays in a student's grade depends upon "what portion of the course goals the portfolio is expected to represent" (Herman, Gearhart, & Aschbacher, 1996, p. 41). Even though various pieces of work may have been graded along the way, teachers may look at the pieces in the portfolio with fresh eyes for evidence of growth and progress.

## RECORDING AND REPORTING RESULTS

In reality, most of the information teachers gather about student learning boils down to a single letter in a grade book or on a report card. How can you ensure that the grades you assign reflect as fairly as possible what a student knows and can do? How can you ensure that students and parents understand the meaning of the grades you assign?

**CCSSO Principle 6: Communication and CCSSO Principle 10: Community**

Guskey (1996) has provided three general guidelines that can help you ensure that your grading and reporting practices are "fair, equitable, and useful to students, parents, and teachers" (p. 20).

1. *Begin with a clear statement of purpose.* This statement should address "why grading and reporting is done, for whom the information is intended, and what the desired results are" (p. 20).
2. *Provide accurate and understandable descriptions of student learning.* Even if this description is reduced to a single letter, students and parents must understand what that letter represents. For example, does a B represent level of achievement only or were other factors, such as attendance or progress, involved in calculating the grade?

3. *Use grading and reporting methods to enhance, not hinder, teaching and learning.* The common practice of averaging can lead to an inaccurate picture of student learning if a student's work demonstrates that past assessment information no longer reflects their learning. The practice of assigning zeros for late or missing work can have a devastating effect on students' grades, especially when averaging is used.

Of all the important decisions you will make as a teacher, decisions about grades can be the most difficult for you and the most significant for your students. If you take this responsibility seriously, you will continue to educate yourself in this area and to reflect often and critically about the grading and reporting practices you employ in your teaching.

## EXTERNAL
## ASSESSMENT AND EVALUATION

High-stakes testing is a critical piece of the standards-based reform movement, which has dominated American education for the past two decades. Tests that carry significant consequences for teachers, schools, and students are referred to as high-stakes tests. Advocates of standards-based reform claim that standards make clear to everyone what needs to be taught and learned and tests hold teachers and schools accountable for teaching it. Critics argue that such policies also lead to a number of undesirable outcomes, including a narrowing of the curriculum, a shift away from teaching untested skills and subjects, and a strong incentive to both teachers and administrators to cheat in various ways (Jacob, 2002). Increased emphasis on test scores may have led to higher test scores, but is the result worth the effort? Are test scores the ultimate purpose of school reform?

It is important to be able to use the data derived from standardized tests to improve instruction. Classroom-level reports allow teachers to see how a group of students performs across the curriculum. Group score reports allow teachers to focus on when content, concepts, and skills are taught and how students are required to demonstrate mastery (Mertler, 2004)

Individual score reports can be used to pinpoint a student's strengths and weaknesses. For example, standardized tests can yield such subscores as "Capitalization," "Punctuation: Commas," and "Math Concepts and Estimation" (Mertler, 2004). With this information, teachers can target where students need help and plan instruction accordingly.

# SUMMARY

Awesome responsibility comes with the power to evaluate others. Carelessly designed assessments and hastily assigned grades may have little effect on students who always perform well academically, but may very well curtail the educational opportunities and life chances of students who are less adept at "doing school." Among the key points to remember are:

- Assessment and evaluation involve gathering information about student learning in order to make relevant instructional decisions.
- Assessments must be as free of bias and as equitable as possible.
- Both traditional and alternative forms of classroom assessment have strengths and limitations and are more appropriate for some purposes than others.
- Assessment practices should enable students to become skilled self-assessors.
- Recording and reporting methods should enhance, not hinder, teaching and learning.
- High-stakes assessment for accountability purposes is a critical piece in the standards-based reform movement.

## *Reflecting on the Standards*

- In your subject area, what would a classroom assessment system look like that fairly reflects what all students know and can do?
- How can you create equitable assessment conditions in your own classroom?
- To what extent should individual, sociocultural, linguistic, and other differences be accommodated in assessment and evaluation?
- What is the value of self-assessment?
- What are the purposes of grades?
- What factors will you consider when assigning grades?
- What is the role of accountability in public education? To whom, if anyone, should teachers be accountable and for what?
- How will you as a teacher react to large-scale, high-stakes testing?

# Part III

# PROFESSIONAL CONTEXTS OF TEACHING

# CHAPTER 11

# Understanding
# the Role of Community

To what communities will you belong as a teacher and how will you participate constructively in them? Often beginning teachers are so overwhelmed
by their many new responsibilities that they neglect cultivating relationships
with other members of the school community. This is understandable but
unfortunate because school administrators, other teachers, community agencies, local businesses, parents, and guardians all play a role in helping you
become a successful teacher.

The overall purpose of this chapter is related to CCSSO Principle #10:
*The teacher fosters relationships with school colleagues, parents, and agencies in the
larger community to support students' learning and well-being.*

Specifically, this chapter will help you:

- Understand schools as organizations within the larger community
  context;
- Become aware of how collegial activities make schools productive
  learning environment;
- Plan for respectful and productive relationships with parents and
  guardians;
- Identify and use community resources to foster student learning.

### REFLECTING ON PRACTICE: LIZ SPALDING–
### "A STORMY START TO THE FIRST YEAR OF TEACHING"

On a late August morning in 1974, I rose after a nearly sleepless night and set
off for my very first day as a teacher. But my jitters turned out to be unneces-
sary. The halls of Valley High School were noticeably uncrowded, and when
the bell sounded the beginning of first period, only five or six students sat scat-
tered about my classroom. As the day progressed, this pattern held. The Kanawha County Textbook Protest was under way in Charleston, West Virginia.

The trouble had begun during the summer over the district's language arts textbook adoptions. For several months the books were on display in public libraries for community review. After the period allotted for public review expired without incident, the books were adopted. But soon a core of political and religious conservatives began fanning the flames of censorship. Angry protesters picketed the Board of Education building, brandishing homemade placards proclaiming "No Dirty Books."

Valley High School (a pseudonym) served a mostly blue-collar community. The largest employers were the chemical and coal industries. Many families lived "up the creek" or "up the hollow." The community was predominantly White and Protestant, and many of the churches were fundamentalist. But it had never occurred to me that this community would be one of the hot spots of the Textbook Protest. Even though I had grown up only 10 miles away, I was as unfamiliar with Valley High's culture as if I had grown up 10,000 miles away.

Textbook protesters, soon joined by coal miners striking in sympathy, began picketing Valley High's parking lot. They didn't stop anyone from entering, but they certainly made us uncomfortable. Although no violence happened at my school, violent incidents did occur elsewhere. A nearby elementary school—empty at the time—was bombed.

James Moffett (1988), the author of the most vilified textbook series in the adoption, explained how textbooks could cause such turmoil. For example, the textbooks were accused of promoting "relativism in language usage," a strategy that Moffett claimed allowed protesters to uphold "proper grammar" while discriminating against "minority dialects in literature selections" (p. 14). One leader of the protest called the books "filthy, trashy, disgusting, one-sidedly in favor of Blacks, and unpatriotic" (p. 15). Protesters paid for full-page newspaper ads featuring "dirty" words and phrases taken out of the context of literature that had been anthologized for years.

Eventually the protest faded from the front page and the majority of the "dirty books" were warehoused. By the second semester, normalcy had returned. Like many young and inexperienced teachers, I was wary of parents. The textbook protest made me even more reluctant to communicate with them and contributed to the general feeling that the school and the community were adversaries, not partners in a common enterprise.

Over the next 5 years, I learned a great deal about the Valley High School community. I sponsored the Latin Club, which met monthly, each time in a different student's home. We held car washes and bake sales to raise money for a trip to Rome. Parents—most of whom were working-class and few of whom had traveled outside West Virginia—paid the bulk of the expenses. They chaperoned and transported students to extracurricular events. They donated money and time to our club's annual service project. Parents were not the enemy but my greatest allies in building a flourishing Latin program at Valley High School.

I now realize that those who attacked the textbooks in Kanawha County were as sincere and passionate in their opposition as those who defended them. The view many teachers and I held at the time–that the educational establishment was enlightened and right and the protesters were ignorant and wrong–is simplistic and biased.

### Questions to Consider

- What values were shared by your school and your community? What values were contested?
- How were your parents and/or other adults involved with your education? How, if at all, did they interact with your teachers?
- How did the schools you attended celebrate their history, traditions, and shared values?

## WHAT IS COMMUNITY?

In the past, traditional communities–schools, congregations, neighborhoods, towns–were relatively homogeneous. They changed little from year to year. They were often suspicious of outsiders and demanded conformity from insiders. Members of traditional communities shared generations of history and continuity. This description no longer fits many contemporary communities, as our population becomes more mobile and the demographics of communities change rapidly.

John Gardner (1995), an American scholar, author, public servant, and activist, offered a new vision of community. He wrote that successful contemporary communities practice a philosophy of pluralism, maintain an open climate for dissent, and offer subcommunities the opportunity to retain their identity and share in the setting of larger group goals. At the same time, there must be institutional arrangements for diminishing polarization, for teaching diverse groups to know one another, for coalition-building, dispute resolution, negotiation, and mediation (p. 169).

Situations in which the values of the public school conflict with the values of individuals and groups are becoming more common as a result of the increasing diversity of this country. As diversity increases in this country, Gardner argued, we must identify shared secular values such as liberty, justice, and tolerance, which transcend religious and cultural differences.

In addition, successful communities foster an atmosphere of cooperation and connectedness. There is a sense of belonging and identity, a spirit of mutual responsibility, altruism, tolerance, and loyalty. Everyone is included; there is room for "mavericks, nonconformists, and dissenters; there are no outcasts" (p. 171). In successful communities, many individuals are willing to share leadership tasks and to speak out on issues of concern. Successful communities reaffirm themselves and build their own morale. They celebrate their history, traditions, and shared values.

Finally, successful communities have mechanisms in place to pass on shared values and leadership to the next generation, to maintain participation, and to resolve conflicts. Many educational reforms fail to survive changes of leadership and personnel precisely because such provisions have not been made.

## SOCIAL CAPITAL AND SCHOOLS
## AS DEMOCRATIC LEARNING COMMUNITIES

In *Bowling Alone: The Collapse and Revival of American Community* (2000), Robert D. Putnam used the sport of bowling to trace the trajectories of individualism and community in the late 20th century: While more Americans are bowling than ever before, "league bowling has plummeted in the last 10 to 15 years" (p. 112). The status of league bowling is paradigmatic of the decline of social capital, "the benefits that individuals and groups derive from active social association" (Wraga, 2002, p. 34).

Social capital is critical to the development and education of children and youth. Putnam's analysis shows that in states where social capital is highest, children flourish and schools are successful. In fact, Putnam goes on to demonstrate that increasing social capital in a state will have a greater effect on educational outcomes than educational reform (e.g., decreasing class size) alone.

Social capital is built through social networks and norms of reciprocity. Reciprocity means doing for others without expecting anything specific back in the expectation that "someone else will do something for me down the road" (p. 21). Teachers can help build social capital in schools by:

- Demonstrating loyalty to the school, seeking innovative approaches to learning, reaching out to parents, and feeling a deep sense of responsibility for students' development;
- Inventing powerful and enticing ways of increasing civic engagement, including participation in the life of the school and community;
- Working together as teams;
- Offering opportunities for students to participate in cultural, economic, and political activities and participating themselves.

Wraga (2002) has outlined ways high schools can generate social capital. First, schools should offer more opportunities for students to take electives that contribute to a well-rounded education and that cut across the increasingly rigid tracks that separate the college-bound from the non-college-bound. Student involvement in extracurricular school activities is another avenue for creating social capital. Finally, high schools should affirm their commitment to fostering a democratic community through their daily operations, such as attention to public spaces, approaches to participatory decision-making, and outreach activities.

## TEACHERS AND COMMUNITIES OF PRACTICE

A community of practice is a form of social capital defined as: ". . . groups of people informally bound together by shared expertise and passion for a joint enterprise . . . . [P]eople in communities of practice share their experiences and knowledge in free-flowing, creative ways that foster new approaches to problems" (Wenger & Snyder, 2000, p. 139). Teacher communities of practice focus on: 1. the improvement of student learning; and 2. the continuing development of the teacher's subject knowledge (Grossman, Wineburg, & Woolworth, 2001).

In high schools with strong professional communities, students have shown gains in engagement and achievement in core subject areas, an effect that was even greater for students who generally achieve at lower levels in school. Teachers who collectively question their own practice, generate solutions to problems, and support one another's growth may be key to instructional improvement and school reform (Cochran-Smith & Lytle, 1996; Little, 2003).

## CONNECTING WITH COMMUNITIES WITHIN A SCHOOL

Although teaching has traditionally been characterized as an isolated profession (Lortie, 1975), more and more educators are realizing the benefits of collegiality. Seymour Sarason (1993) described the personal satisfaction that can be derived from one's peers:

**CCSSO Principle 9: Reflection**

> There are many things money can't buy, and one of them is the sense that you are continuing to experience the sense of growth with and from children and with and from colleagues. Over the long run, it is these two senses that keep you willingly engaged in your work. (p. 67)

In this section, you will be introduced to several ways teachers work collegially.

## Subject Departments

Research on secondary school teaching reveals that the colleagues who matter most are the members of one's subject department. Even when schools restructure into "houses" or interdisciplinary teams, teachers tend to retain their identity as subject specialists and to see the subject department as their professional home (Siskin & Little, 1995). Ideally, subject departments are cohesive and collegial, although they can be fragmented and contentious. Teachers in collegial departments share materials and plans, visit one another's classrooms, share responsibility for leading the department, and mentor newcomers.

## Middle School Teams

Many middle schools organize students and teachers into interdisciplinary teams. Middle school teams share the same group of students, the same part of a building, and the same schedule and planning time. These are the foundations of teamwork. The actual work of a team

| CCSSO Principle 3: Adapting Instruction |

falls into four categories. First, teams share common methods of organization. They collaboratively develop and enforce team rules and procedures. They share a common approach to communicating with parents and to using school time. Second, they actively work on community-building. They accomplish this through developing team names, mottoes, and symbols. They plan and implement units as a team, produce team publications, and stage a variety of group activities. Third, they teach as a team. They plan together and implement interdisciplinary instruction either along parallel courses or in integrated blocks. Finally, a team has some form of self-governance and is represented in the governance of the school (Hackmann, Petzko, Valentine, Clark, Nori, & Lucas, 2002).

## Collaborative Classrooms

Many schools use the designation *collaborative* for classrooms in which general education and special education teachers work together to meet the needs of all students. This is perhaps the most challenging collegial relationship of all. Historically, teachers have had no need to negotiate teaching tasks, procedures, or rules. Collaborative classrooms, on the other hand, include at least two certified teachers and often at least one paraprofessional.

Two teachers who collaborate effectively have given the following tips for success:

- Teach together. One teacher might lead discussion, while the other records on the whiteboard.
- Use space productively. If the special education teacher's classroom is empty, use it for a quiet space or for conferences.
- Capitalize on each other's strengths.
- Be positive role models of how to handle disagreements respectfully.
- Stand together on discipline.
- Plan together (Kimbrell-Lee & Wood, 1994).

## CONNECTING WITH COMMUNITIES BEYOND THE SCHOOL

For many middle and high schools, involving parents and the community has become a top priority (Brandt, 1998), in part because of changing student and family demographics. Many parents and families of young people in school today do not speak English or speak English minimally and may have had little or no experience with formal education.

**CCSSO Principle 3: Adapting Instruction**

In many immigrant families, the school-age children are their connection to American culture. Often, middle and high school students serve as translators for their parents and extended families. Family configurations have changed greatly as well, and a large number of children are growing up in nontraditional families.

King and Goodwin (2002) have detailed seven culturally responsive strategies teachers and administrators can use to engage parents and other caring adults. These strategies include:

- Express a commitment to culturally responsive parental involvement in mission statements and goals;
- Survey parents' perspectives, concerns, and ideas;
- Offer parent-teacher seminars and activities based on survey results;
- Appoint a school/family liaison;
- Develop a school cultural resources binder;
- Create a space/room for families to meet, read, talk, and relax;
- As a community, generate multiple ways to involve parents in and inform them about the school. Commit to at least two of these.

Parents of students at Loganville High School in Loganville, Georgia, come to the school at least once a year to discuss the plan for what their children will do during their years in high school and after they graduate. Parents volunteer their time and expertise in a variety of ways at the school. Parental involvement as part of a comprehensive reform plan has helped Loganville High School students dramatically increase attendance, persistence, and the pursuit of education beyond high school (Gest, 2000).

## Communicating Successfully with Parents and Guardians

As a beginning teacher, you may feel some anxiety about communicating with parents and guardians. Yet, research consistently shows that children with involved parents do better in school and are more successful in life (http://www.ptacentral. org). How can you help increase the involvement of the significant adults in students' lives? When asked, parents consistently voice three broad concerns. How much does a teacher know and care about 1. teaching? 2. my child? 3. communicating with me? (Rich, 1998). The following guidelines can help you communicate effectively with parents and guardians.

| CCSSO Principle 6: |
| Effective |
| Communication |

- Communicate your knowledge of and enthusiasm for teaching and students.
- Show you know your students, understand how they learn, and value them as individuals.
- Put yourself in the shoes of the parent and empathize that parents have a tough job.
- Use plain language rather than education terminology.
- Demonstrate that your expectations for behavior are fair, consistent, and respectful.
- Demonstrate that your academic expectations are high yet attainable.
- Show interest in parents' views of and goals for the student.
- Be accessible and responsive to parents.
- Contact parents promptly with any behavioral and/or academic concerns and persist in trying to build relationships.
- Be the bearer of good news as well as bad
  (Davern, 1996; Giannett & Sagarese, 1998; Rich, 1998).

Even if parents cannot demonstrate their engagement by coming to the school, their engagement at home remains important. Two broad categories of parental engagement at home are associated with school performance: 1. holding high expectations for a student's school success; and 2. providing a supportive home environment (Thorkildsen & Scott Stein, 1998). You can encourage parental engagement at home by communicating your academic expectations, by suggesting how parents can help students achieve course goals, by encouraging them to talk with their children about school, by inviting them to review and comment on student work, and even by involving them in projects and assignments (Finn, 1998).

Conferencing with parents/guardians is part of your professional responsibility. Most middle and high schools have some regularly scheduled times for parent conferences. Sometimes either you or the parent/guardian of a student will request a conference. Whatever the purpose of the conference, being prepared for it will give you confidence in your professionalism.

### Theory into Practice: Back to School Night

Britt Morgan (a pseudonym) wrote the following reflective vignette during her first year of teaching in a large urban high school. As you read, think about what you have read about involving parents/guardians in their children's education and then answer the questions that follow.

Back to School Night ended and I immediately began to cry. I had spent all afternoon getting the classroom ready. I put up some of the students' work, I made sure each desk was neatly in its place, and I even cleaned the whiteboard so it would shine. Three weeks into my first year of teaching and I hadn't shed a single tear. Now, I couldn't help but cry.

At 7 p.m. I stood at the door and I waited, and I waited, and I waited. First period passed. Second, third, fourth, and no one came. I stood at that door and felt like such a fool. I felt naive for thinking I'd have a room full of parents each period listening and questioning what I was going to teach their children that year.

By 9 p.m. I had one father show. One father for over 120 students. He and his son Pierce arrived late to my scheduled presentation for sixth period, which consisted of me sitting and waiting for someone, anyone to arrive. I'd long since thrown out the note cards I'd written to myself reminding me of my presentation highlights and erased the large "Welcome Parents" I'd written on the whiteboard.

But Pierce and his dad made Back to School Night important. I realized on that night that sometimes in teaching it's not about the 120 kids, it's about the one student. Pierce's dad asked how he could help at home and what Pierce should be working on to make sure he was on top of his assignments. He said he was a single father and worked long hours, but they had just moved here and he wanted to make sure Pierce was succeeding in school. And right before Pierce and his dad left, Pierce gave me a hug.

I couldn't help but think, "My gosh! I've known this kid for 3 weeks, he's a 15-year-old boy and he just hugged his teacher in front of his father." Maybe for the past 3 weeks I had been doing something right after all. First-year teaching is full of questioning your lesson plans, your overall goals, and your sanity. We rise early and stay late—just to make sure that one kid gets it. But Pierce's hug confirmed it all. I was meant to be there.

I cried that night because I was angry. No one had prepared me for this moment. In my own world, parents showed up for Back to School Night. I didn't want to live in a world where parents couldn't or wouldn't show. Or even worse, a kid didn't have parents. I cried that night out of fear I wasn't going to connect with my students because of the different worlds we lived in. I doubted myself because my lack of hardships as a child might further distance me from my kids. But the only thing I could let get in the way was my own fear.

I realize now that Back to School Night was just one night. It is my job to use the rest of the year to invest my students and their families in my class. But I am still thankful for that night. Because the reality is that teaching is full of moments that humble us to tears.

***Questions to Consider.*** Sadly, Britt's experience with Back to School night is not unusual. Thus, many teachers are left with the impression that parents and caregivers don't care about students' learning in school. This leads to a very unhelpful blame game. There are many legitimate reasons why Back to School nights may not be well attended. Luckily for Britt, Pierce and his dad showed up. Britt learned an important lesson that night and Pierce's academic career was most likely influenced.

- Can you think of some reasons why Back to School nights may not be well attended, especially by the parents and caregivers who most need to be there?
- How do you react to Britt's statement, "I cried that night out of fear I wasn't going to connect with my students because of the different worlds we lived in"?
- What are some ways Britt can go about using "the rest of the year to invest my students and their families in my class"?

## When Community Members Disagree

Despite your knowledge, training, and best efforts to communicate, parents or guardians may disagree with your classroom practices or selection of instructional materials. What should you do when you receive complaints? First, you should be familiar with district or school policies on this issue. These policies should be shared with parents and can be used to resolve conflicts. You should also check with your subject area professional organization to see whether the organization has a statement about censorship or dealing with controversial issues and what support they offer to teachers.

> **CCSSO Principle 7: Planning**

Willis (1995) suggests the following guidelines to help you avoid or minimize conflicts.

- Seek community input before selecting books and other texts. If you know a topic is controversial, consider forming an advisory committee that represents a range of perspectives.
- Have a written policy and procedures for dealing with complaints.
- If a protest should occur, focus on how the community was involved in the selection process, the content of the book, and how it is used in your classroom.
- Remember that curriculum must reflect the knowledge of experts and scholars as well as the culture of the community.
- Acknowledge that context doesn't necessarily legitimize all offenses. For example, parents or guardians may be offended by certain words or images regardless of their educational value.
- Be professional in providing alternative assignments for students whose parents/guardians disagree with your choice of texts.

## Connecting with Communities Through Service and Work

More and more middle and high schools are reconnecting with communities by expanding the services they offer, embedding service to the community in the school curriculum, and enlisting the help of business and industry in preparing students for employment and careers.

> **CCSSO Principle 2: Learning and Human Development**

*Full-service schools* aspire to be "one-stop centers where the educational, physical, psychological, and social requirements of students and their families are addressed in a rational, holistic fashion" (Dryfoos, 1996, p. 18). Intermediate School 218 in New York City is an example of a full-service school. It opens at 7:00 a.m. to offer breakfast and activities to students and remains open until 10:00 p.m. to offer enrichment, sports, and workshops for students and members of the community. The school also offers weekend and summer programs. A Family Resource Center offers social services, and there is a health and dental clinic on site.

Many schools and individual teachers are implementing *service learning* as an immediate way to reconnect schools and communities. Service learning seeks to "promote students' self-esteem, to develop higher order thinking skills, to make use of multiple abilities, and to provide authentic learning experiences—all goals of current curriculum reform efforts" (Kahne & Westheimer, 1996, p. 592). In addition, service learning projects offer students the opportunity to practice citizenship while meeting community needs. Service learning projects may involve students in analyzing environmental issues, compiling and publishing an oral history of the community, tutoring younger students, or working with the homeless. When service learning is integrated into the curriculum, both academic and social goals can be met. For example, art students at Spring Harbor Middle School in Madison, Wisconsin, became interested in supporting Habitat for Humanity. As a class, they decided to raise money for Habitat by collecting, restoring, and decorating old chairs for resale. The chairs symbolized the comforts of home. The classroom teacher provided lessons in color, design, and painting techniques, while the students also practiced interpersonal and written communication skills in organizing and conducting a silent auction of the completed chairs at a local mall (Petto, 1998). Service learning can be integrated into any subject, and students of all ages are capable of contributing to the welfare of their community.

*School-community partnerships* hold great promise for improving the outcomes of schooling. These partnerships are usually between a business and a school. Multiple partnerships with multiple objectives may exist in a single school. For example, a team of researchers studied how partnerships functioned in one large urban high school in Houston, Texas (Scales, Foster, Mannes, Horst, Pinto, & Rutherford, 2005). Some of the programs within the school were geared toward high-achieving students; others were created to help students with low socioeconomic status and less academic accomplishment. The programs offered many kinds of help ranging from putting information about scholarships into the hands of students, to providing academic and professional mentoring, to building strong relationships with students and involving their families in the education process. The researchers concluded, "[T]hese partnerships appear to have opened the doors of learning for students who otherwise may not have done either so well in high school, or formulated plans to pursue higher education" (p. 185).

Finally, *school-to-work programs* seek to meet the academic and occupational aspirations of a broad range of students. Many high schools now offer career "academies" through which students explore employment opportunities in health care, travel and tourism, public safety, or technical fields. While studying academic subjects, students in school-to-work programs also complete paid or unpaid internships and assume job responsibilities under the guidance of a worksite mentor. The goal is for students to leave high school with authentic problem-solving skills in a given field; a realistic idea of the opportunities and constraints offered by a particular career path; an appreciation of the link between academic and workplace learning; and connections to adult practitioners and, eventually, to employment (Goldberger & Kazis, 1996).

The initiatives described above are indicative of educators' growing consciousness that schools and communities must work in partnership to address the changing intellectual, social, emotional, and physical needs of today's middle and high school students. Just as the image of the teacher as an isolated expert dispensing knowledge to passive learners is changing, so too is the image of the middle or high school as an efficient and impersonal factory. Today, many businesses are adopting policies and implementing practices that address the complex human needs of their employees. Schools, perhaps more than any other institution, have the potential for creating caring communities in which all members can acquire and practice the skills needed to sustain our sense of common humanity in a rapidly changing world.

## SUMMARY

When you begin teaching, you may be tempted to shut your classroom door and keep your problems and your questions to yourself. You may be reluctant to initiate dialogue with parents and other concerned adults. It is not too early to begin thinking of yourself as a member of a school community. As you begin your work in schools, you can contribute to the creation and maintenance of a vital and thriving community of teachers and learners.

Among the key points to remember are:

- Successful contemporary communities balance wholeness and diversity, share core values, practice participatory democracy, and continually reaffirm and renew themselves.
- While teaching has historically been an isolated profession, collaboration and teamwork increasingly characterize teaching today.
- Collaboration is essential to successful departments, teams, and inclusive classrooms.

- Teachers must plan for and invite parent/guardian involvement.
- Most parental and community conflicts can be resolved through good communication, listening, and negotiation.
- School-community partnerships hold great promise for improving the outcomes of schooling.

### *Reflecting on the Standards*

- How does the community influence who the students are?
- What aspects of students are most relevant to their school performance?
- What are some ways you can recognize whether students are having difficulty in the following areas: cognitive, emotional, social, physical?
- How do you plan to involve parents and other caring adults in your curricular and/or extracurricular activities?
- What students' rights should you consider when working with other adults to improve students' educational experience?
- To what extent are teachers obligated to respect and preserve community values, especially when they may conflict with teachers' personal values?

# CHAPTER 12

# Reflecting for Professional Renewal

When you graduate from your teacher preparation program and step into your own classroom, you will quickly learn that a great deal of responsibility rests on your shoulders. Assistance will be available, but you will be expected to take the initiative in becoming a professional. You have the core knowledge: learning from your education classes, observations, student teaching experiences, and interactions with teachers and teacher educators. Now you will need to do the rest.

This chapter gives an overview of some of the opportunities for growth that will be available to you as you enter and move forward in your career. This book concludes with emphasis on the same CCSSO standard (#9) we highlighted in Chapter 1: *The teacher is a reflective practitioner who continually evaluates the effects of his/her choices and actions on others (students, parents, and other professionals in the learning community) and who actively seeks out opportunities to grow professionally.*

Specifically, this chapter will help you:

- Become familiar with resources available for professional learning;
- Seek out professional literature, colleagues, and other resources to support your own development as a learner and teacher;
- Articulate the purpose and value of mentoring and induction programs
- Make use of networks and support groups to give and receive help;
- Become aware of the many opportunities for lifelong learning through participation in higher education and professional associations;
- Reflect on your course learning and your future as a teacher.

### *REFLECTING ON PRACTICE:* LIZ SPALDING–"MOVING BEYOND THE APPRENTICESHIP OF OBSERVATION"

Despite the fact that I had completed an accredited teacher education program at a highly regarded university, when I entered teaching I was a victim of the *apprenticeship of observation.* This term was coined by Lortie (1975), who proposed that prospective teachers have learned a great deal about teaching before they ever enter the profession as a result of many years of sitting in classrooms as students and observing teaching. For some individuals, the apprenticeship of observation is so powerful that teacher education programs have very little effect on their thinking about teaching. In my case, Sister Judith's style (described in Chapter 1) had become so firmly fixed in my mind that I emulated her without even realizing it. Only after 9 years of classroom teaching did I finally have a professional development experience that enabled me to move beyond this apprenticeship.

For years I had been frustrated with teaching writing. Despite my assiduous efforts at assigning and evaluating essays, most students glanced at their grades, then crumpled up the papers and deposited them in the trash can or on the classroom floor. I jumped at the opportunity to participate in a summer institute–the Bay Area Writing Project at the University of California, Berkeley.

I was perplexed when I received in the mail information about preparation for the workshop: I was supposed to write a personal narrative and bring it with me. I taught people to write; I didn't *actually* write! Ever a dutiful student, I completed the assignment, all the while worrying about who would grade it and what grade I would receive. At the institute, we broke into small groups, read our papers aloud, and gave feedback to one another about our writing. Then we revised our papers. I never did receive a grade on that paper, but it improved markedly with revision based on my peers' feedback. Over the course of the institute, we teachers wrote and shared our writing every day; observed other teachers demonstrating their best practices in teaching writing; and read, reflected on, and discussed thought-provoking texts. The light came on: All these years, I had just been assigning writing, *not* teaching it!

The Bay Area Writing Project, a site of the National Writing Project that today has hundreds of sites in the United States and abroad, revolutionized my teaching. I couldn't wait to get back to my classroom to try out all the new techniques I had learned. I discovered that the quality of my students' writing improved immensely when I gave them choices of topics and approaches to writing, responsibility for helping one another through peer review, and an opportunity to revise their writing based on concrete feedback from me and others. These techniques were especially helpful for those students who were still struggling to master written English. My students experienced success and so did I.

I still admire Sister Judith for her knowledge of literature, her passion for teaching it, and the high standards she held for her students. But from my experience in the Bay Area Writing Project, I learned that there is much more to teaching than knowing one's subject. Good teachers are reflective about their practice, have a can-do approach to problem solving, and seek out opportunities to improve their knowledge and skills. They are eager to learn more about their craft, through formal study, through involvement in professional organizations and networks, and through purposeful interactions with colleagues.

One of the principal reasons I have remained a teacher for over 30 years is a selfish one: Every day I learn something new. Every class is different, every student is different, every year is different. I relish the opportunity to change and grow with every course I teach and to learn from my colleagues who are teachers and researchers. Along with all its other rewards, teaching enables me to be a lifelong learner.

### Questions to Consider

- As you think about becoming a teacher, how do you see yourself 5 years from now? Ten years from now?
- What attracts you to teaching?
- What experience do you have participating in support groups, networks, or professional associations?

## DEVELOPING A DISPOSITION FOR REFLECTION

*Disposition* refers to "professional attitudes, values, and beliefs demonstrated through both verbal and non-verbal behaviors as educators interact with students, families, colleagues, and communities" (National Council for the Accreditation of Teacher Education, quoted in Osguthorpe, 2008, p. 290). A teacher education program provides you with core knowledge for *becoming* a professional teacher. This disposition for *becoming* rather than *being* means that you view a teacher education program as providing knowledge that needs further reconstruction as you attempt to understand self, subject area, pedagogy, students, and schools. When you enter the classroom, you add to this core knowledge with insights you gain from your teaching experiences and knowledge you acquire from professional activities, such as exploring the literature in your teaching field, conversing with colleagues, and learning more about your personal and teaching selves. The end remains a goal you are continually pursuing: becoming a professional.

A disposition for reflection will allow you to be analytical in classroom decision making—the processes you use to identify an issue or problem and the approaches you use to solve it. Rousseau and Tate (2003) highlighted the importance of reflection on equity in school mathematics instruction. They studied seven low-track mathematics teachers at the same high school. Students of color were overrepresented in the low-track classes; all seven of the teachers were White. The researchers found that the teachers viewed equity as equal treatment of all students and that they saw themselves as color-blind. Consequently, they failed to question their own practices, such as "allowing students to fail." Yet, the students who were allowed to fail were disproportionately African American males. The researchers noted that true reflection demands questioning assumptions and beliefs and concluded "true reflection in this case was prevented by the teachers' views of justice and by their disposition toward colorblindness" (p. 215). They posed four questions to serve as a beginning framework to assist teacher reflection on equity and instructional practice:

- Is the goal of equal treatment of students an appropriate standard to guide (subject-area) instruction?
- Is a color blind perspective on classroom practice an appropriate view to guide (subject-area) instruction?
- How do students' linguistic, ethnic, racial, and socioeconomic backgrounds influence their (subject-area) learning?
- What is the role of (subject-area) in society and why is this important for students of various cultural backgrounds? (p. 216).

Teachers who are reflective practitioners demonstrate: 1. tolerance for the ambiguity of complex problems; 2. the ability to identify problems of practice and to generate tentative solutions; 3. a willingness to examine their own knowledge and actions; 4. the ability to draw upon intuitive knowledge to solve problems; and 5. the inclination to implement and evaluate new procedures (Vacca, Vacca, & Bruneau, 1997).

Reflective professionals know that there are many ways to look at problems and issues and that explanations and solutions are just as numerous. They also have learned that to increase success in the classroom and to grow professionally, they must be willing to look at themselves and at other variables that may affect what they do in the classroom.

## BECOMING AN ACTION RESEARCHER

Reflection goes hand-in-hand with becoming an action researcher. Teachers who engage in action research "collect data or information for the purpose of solving a practical problem in an authentic setting" (Nolen & Vander Putten, 2007, p. 406). Action research has its roots in the work of Dewey and others who argued for teacher preparation programs that integrate knowledge and action and encourage preservice teachers to become inquirers who use rational methods for exploring problems of practice.

Today the action research movement has strong supporters among teacher educators and K–12 classroom teachers. Action research encourages teachers to see themselves as autonomous professionals who are able to uncover new knowledge that can challenge current perceptions and offer fresh perspectives on learning in contemporary classrooms. Cochran-Smith and Lytle (1993) divide the area of action research (also called teacher research) into two general categories: empirical and theoretical. *Empirical research* originates from observable classroom phenomena and entails collecting, analyzing, and interpreting data. There are many examples of empirical teacher research projects available both online and in journals. For example, George Mason University hosts a website with extensive resources for teacher research, including examples of teacher and action research projects (http://gse.gmu. edu/research/tr). *Conceptual research* refers to the exploration and analysis of ideas. One example of this type of research is a group of seven educators in Alabama who called themselves TRELLIS: Teacher Researchers Expanding Learning, Linking Institutions, Schools (Christensen, Wilson, Anders, Dennis, Kirkland, Beacham, & Warren, 2001). These educators explored how their beliefs about teaching and learning in the social studies had been shaped over their years of teaching. Over a 2-year period, the group members used reflective writing, classroom observation notes, interviews, and videotapes in order to gain a better understanding of their perspective on social studies instruction. As a result, the teachers remodeled their traditional teaching methods and enacted more flexible thinking about their teaching, becoming more effective and innovative social studies practitioners.

Powell, Zehm, and Garcia (1996) identified five phases of the action research cycle: 1. description and speculation; 2. exploration; 3. discovery; 4. reflection and modification; 5. description and speculation. Using this model, let's see how one teacher used action research to solve a problem in her Algebra I class.

An experienced teacher, Susan Martinez (a pseudonym) was hired for a part-time mathematics position at an urban high school with a large enrollment of African Americans and students from a lower socioeconomic status. Having previously taught in a suburban, predominantly White, middle-class high school, she was having trouble adjusting to her new position. She enrolled in a graduate course at a nearby university in order to update her teaching credentials. Conducting an action research project was one of the course requirements.

In the *description/speculation* phase of her research, Susan decided to focus on discipline in a particular class that was giving her difficulties. During the *exploration* phase of her research—about a month—she kept a journal, noting daily events in each class and especially the class on which she was focused. She studied student records in order to construct profiles of the students in each of her algebra classes. She asked a colleague to observe her teaching, to note patterns of disruption, and to record how she handled disruptions. She administered a survey to her students in order to get their input on what was causing discipline problems in the class.

During the ongoing *discovery* phase of her research, she discovered that the problem was not really discipline at all. Yes, a few troublemakers were clearly identified in her colleague's observation, but the real problem was student learning. She discovered that many of the students in this class were repeating algebra. Thus, students differed greatly in motivation, skill, and maturity, and even age. From the student surveys and subsequent class discussions, Susan found that many of the students did not learn well from her style of teaching. While she preferred to work numerous illustrative problems on the board, a number of students said they could not concentrate when she did this. They preferred to work problems quietly at their seats.

Having examined all the data, Susan changed her classroom instruction—the *reflection and modification* phase of her research. She began using heterogeneous cooperative groups, mixing students with different levels of motivation and maturity. She gave students choices for solving problems: Those who wished could cluster around her when she worked problems at the board; others could work independently at their seats. Her discipline problems almost disappeared as a result of these changes. Furthermore, her research project affected her own attitude toward the class. She stepped back and took an analytical approach, viewing the situation as a problem to be solved, not a struggle for control.

In the final phase of *description and speculation,* Susan considered what she had learned from her research and decided to make journal-keeping and regular feedback from students a permanent part of her teaching. She grew curious about gender differences in students' learning of mathematics and about the performance of minority students in her classes. Today Susan continues to study her classroom practices, illustrating how even a small-scale action research project can improve conditions for teaching and learning.

## MENTORING AND INDUCTION PROGRAMS

Mentor, a character in Homer's *Odyssey,* was the wise and trusted friend whom Odysseus left in charge of his household during his travels. In its broadest sense, a mentor is someone who takes special interest in helping another person develop into a successful professional. Mentors are critical players in induction programs, which are designed to help beginning teachers succeed.

The National Commission on Teaching and America's Future (2003) called for "support systems through which every novice teacher is formally

> CCSSO Principle 10: Community

linked to an accomplished teacher and a team of educators who are responsible—and accountable— for his or her success" (p. 27). Whether you enter teaching in a state that offers a formal mentoring program or one that does not, you should know how to recognize a good mentor and how to be a good mentee.

Novice teachers can learn much from mentors: how to organize units, develop lesson plans, employ a variety of teaching strategies, and other skills related to sound pedagogy. In addition, a mentor can help one develop dispositions for a reflective approach to standards-based teaching: introspection, a willingness to admit mistakes and seek help, acceptance of constructive criticism, adoption of an analytical approach to classroom problems, and recognition that becoming an excellent teacher is a lifelong process. The best mentors are those who model the thinking and behavior that you need to understand in order to become an effective and reflective teacher (Tatum & McWhorter, 1999; Wang & Odell, 2002).

Some professional organizations have launched online mentoring initiatives, designed to benefit both new and experienced teachers with features such as an online "teachers' lounge," teaching ideas, interactive discussions, and "cyber-mentors" (McCullough, 1999). A number of other listservs and websites are geared to beginning teachers.

New teacher support groups can "offer a safe place where beginning teachers can voice their concerns, share their joys and frustrations, and help one another deal with problems" (Rogers & Babinski, 1999 p. 38). New teacher support groups, usually sponsored by states or districts, convene regularly to engage in group problem solving. Often an outside facilitator helps participants work through the problems they bring to the table. New teachers can play an important role in supporting one another through the beginning years of teaching.

Teacher study groups are active in many schools. Teacher study groups are usually teacher-directed and self-selected. Teachers who participate in study groups generally identify professional books or articles to read and discuss at regular meetings with an eye toward putting the ideas into practice. Informal groups of teachers who meet to share common interests, such as reading or sports, can also be a great source of support.

Teacher networks provide another avenue for professional growth and collegiality. Teacher networks are diverse in their participants and purposes.

The Foxfire Teacher Outreach Network promotes a place-based curriculum and pedagogy and reaches out to rural teachers. There are also subject-specific networks, such as the Urban Mathematics Collaborative and the National Writing Project (Lieberman & McLaughlin, 1996).

## PROFESSIONAL ASSOCIATIONS AND HIGHER EDUCATION

Professional associations provide many opportunities for networking, learning, and activism. General professional education organizations have a broad base of membership. The membership of subject-area professional organizations consists primarily of teachers in a specific field.

The American Federation of Teachers (AFT) and the National Education Association (NEA) are organizations concerned with the status of teaching, learning, and education in general. These organizations keep abreast of national and state initiatives, pending legislation, and other matters relating to education. They monitor and advocate for improving teachers' working conditions. At the local level, they may be involved in salary negotiations, contract disputes, and other related issues. They also attempt to introduce initiatives and influence legislation related to curriculum, certification, teacher and student evaluation, and other professional issues. Many colleges and universities have local chapters of these organizations that provide services to preservice teachers.

> **CCSSO Principle 10: Community**

Kappa Delta Pi is a national education honor society with chapters across the country. Selection to Kappa Delta Pi is based on high academic achievement, a commitment to education, and a professional attitude that assures steady growth in the profession. The organization sponsors scholarships for future teachers, grants for classroom teachers, and community service projects. The organization also publishes many resources for teachers.

Subject-specific professional organizations, such as the National Council for the Social Studies (NCSS), the National Council of Teachers of Mathematics (NCTM), and the National Council of Teachers of English (NCTE), offer many benefits to preservice and inservice teachers. Among them are: access to journals and books published by the organization; opportunity to attend state and national conferences at discounted rates; opportunity to network with other professionals in your field; and access to forums, such as electronic discussion groups, on current and enduring issues in the teaching of your subject. Preservice teachers can attend workshops and local, state, and national meetings and learn first-hand about their subject area and education as a profession. Table 12.1 gives contact information for selected subject-area organizations.

TABLE 12.1. Links to Selected Professional Subject Area Associations

| Subject Area | Organization | Web Link |
|---|---|---|
| The Arts | Music Teachers National Association | http://www.mtna.org |
| Business | National Business Education Association | http://www.nbea.org |
| Civics and Government | The Center for Civic Education | http://www.civiced.org |
| Economics | National Council on Economic Education | http://www.ncee.net |
| Foreign Language | American Council on the Teaching of Foreign Languages | http://www.actfl.org |
| Geography | National Council for Geographic Education | http://www.ncge.org |
| Health/ Physical Education | American Alliance for Health, Physical Education, Recreation and Dance | http://www.aahperd.org |
| History | National Center for History in the School | http://nchs.ucla.edu |
| Language Arts/ Reading | International Reading Association | http://www.reading.org |
| English | National Council of Teachers of English | http://www.ncte.org |
| Mathematics | National Council of Teachers of Mathematics | http://www.nctm.org |
| Science | National Science Teachers Association | http://www.nsta.org |
| Social Studies | National Council for the Social Studies | http://www.ncss.org |
| Teaching English as a Second Language | Teachers of English to Speakers of Other Languages | http://www.tesol.org |
| Technology Education | International Technology Education Association | http://www.iteaconnect.org |

The teacher quality provisions of No Child Left Behind (NCLB) have already sent many practicing teachers scurrying back to school to earn credits to enhance their knowledge and skills (U.S. Department of Education, 2003). Whether or not taking subject-matter courses and passing multiple-choice tests of subject-matter knowledge actually do increase teacher quality is debatable (Berry, Hoke, & Hirsch, 2004). Regardless of current federal policy, however, you will probably continue taking courses in higher education after you graduate from your current program.

Smagorinsky, Cook, and Johnson (2003) promote the idea that a university should serve as a practitioner's conceptual home base–"a community of practice whose ideas are powerful enough to inspire ideological loyalty and enduring, if ever-developing, beliefs about teaching" (p. 1420). Conventional wisdom has it that theory resides at the university, far removed from the front lines of practice, but Smagorinsky, Cook, and Johnson reject this binary, arguing that it does not at all reflect how people learn.

## Theory into Practice: Reflection on Professional Growth

Below is a reflective vignette written by Maggie Wilde (a pseudonym), a middle school teacher, as she completed her master's degree program in secondary education. As you read, think about how Maggie has engaged in professional renewal.

As a direct result of my desire to better reach and understand my students and become a better, more informed teacher, I enrolled in an M.Ed. program at the University of Nevada Las Vegas. I continued teaching full-time while conducting my studies, and I finally earned my master's degree in December of 2005. Up to that point in my teaching career, my experience had been in high school English and Adult E.L.L. I loved teaching these subjects, but due to a serious auto accident, I was forced to take time off from the teaching profession. Upon recuperation, I worked in the public sector for a few years and then ultimately decided that I missed teaching, terribly.

I applied for and happily accepted a middle school position with the Clark County School District (CCSD) in Las Vegas to teach both Study Skills and English to 8th graders. Having been out of the school hallways for so long, I was nervous, yet thrilled at the prospect of working with students again. I thought to myself, "Piece of cake! The 8th graders have to be easier to deal with than those high schoolers of mine, and I'll bet the workload is much less, too!" I was to learn, however, that my expectations were not realistic.

Teaching, on any level, requires that teachers foster students' self-esteem, motivation, character, civic responsibility and their respect for individual, cultural, religious and racial differences. However, I have learned that early adolescents share certain characteristics, such as being easily led and tending to follow dominant practices and beliefs, both at home and within their peer groups. My teaching passion has increasingly become being more involved with my students' cultures and backgrounds, while providing quality instruction and using more up-to-date research, pedagogy, and technology.

I strive to create a classroom climate that is welcoming to diverse cultures and interests. My students continually showcase their cultural works in various formats. For example, this year they put together a time capsule that they sealed at the beginning of the school year and will open at the end of May, to commemorate their rite of passage from middle to high school. Students added cultural artifacts to their capsules and have discussed their culture and interests in their writing and classroom discussions. We also use the Internet to conduct research on topics within the curriculum and topics that arise as a part of classroom discussions. I can tell you, these eighth graders really can show you a thing or two about computers! It is a real pleasure to see students who would normally not want to read ("Ack! Read a book? No way!") zip through websites and find even more information than was originally required.

My experience supervising a group of at-risk students who wanted to produce a talent show illustrates the need for fostering students' academic as well as social skills. The students approached me with the idea, so I gave them a chance (they were previously banned from extracurricular activities due to poor behavior and low grades). In return, we devised a contract (to be signed by the students, their parents or guardians, and me) stating that they would maintain or improve their grades and behavior, as well as improve their citizenship grades. What started out as an after-school activity turned into a truly collaborative effort between the student body and faculty. This diverse group of students took a huge risk and ultimately put on an amazing performance. Had I not been cognizant of the fact that my students needed someone to believe in them and to demand a lot of them, I doubt they would have had that chance to shine. I am truly honored to have been a part of their success.

As I grow in my experience and see more and more opportunity to reach my middle school students, I know that I am learning just as much as they are, if not more. My graduate studies have greatly influenced my practice, because the knowledge I gained helped me develop my lessons, improve my interactions with my students, and cultivate a deeper awareness of my students' needs. Our students live in a different age; if we are not willing to keep up with the changing contexts, if we do not reach out and try to understand them, then how can they truly learn to value education or themselves?

*Questions to Consider.* In earning a master's degree in education, Maggie was required to take courses in a number of areas, including adolescent psychology, multicultural education, contemporary literature for adolescents, conducting action research, and curriculum in middle and secondary schools.

- What might Maggie have learned in her master's degree program that helped her to be a better teacher?
- What evidence does Maggie give that she is a reflective practitioner?
- What evidence suggests that Maggie knows how to put theory into practice?
- How does Maggie know she is making a difference in her students' lives?

## NATIONAL BOARD FOR PROFESSIONAL TEACHING STANDARDS

Historically, intellectually curious teachers like Maggie have had few opportunities or incentives to hone their craft while staying in the classroom. Many found that the only career ladder available led them out of the classroom and into administration. Financial rewards for teaching have been based primarily upon longevity and/or acquiring graduate credit hours in education. Now that Maggie has finished her master's degree program, she is looking at the next step in her professional growth, certification by the National Board for Professional Teaching Standards (NBPTS).

Launched in 1987, the NBPTS offers a voluntary certification process that includes self-evaluations, portfolios, student work, reflection on teaching, and subject-matter tests (Jacobson, 2004, p. 1). Teachers who complete and pass this rigorous process are certified as accomplished teachers and recognized and rewarded in different ways by different states and districts.

Many states, districts, and education organizations are encouraging teachers at all grade levels and in all subject areas for which advanced certification has been developed to take on this challenge. In many cases, teachers receive guidance on how best to prepare for the rigorous assessments and financial support to pay the costs of the process. While some critics have questioned the expense of the process, researchers recently completed a large-scale study that showed that nationally certified teachers in the United States were significantly more effective at raising their students' reading and math scores than teachers who attempted but failed to receive the certification (Jacobson, 2004).

## COMPILING A TEACHING PORTFOLIO

If you are reading this book and enrolled in a teacher education program, it is likely that you are also in the process of compiling a portfolio that will ultimately demonstrate what you know and can do as a teacher. We have designed the content and questions in this book to help you create your own educational autobiography and an initial educational philosophy that show who you are becoming as a teacher.

An autobiography is a portrayal of self. It describes your past and present experiences and tells how these experiences have influenced your process of becoming a teacher. It should also relate some of your interactions with adults and adolescents and reveal your perceptions about education and schooling. You may wish to include summaries of and reflections on your experiences with diversity and education, curriculum and the use of the textbook in the classroom, technology in schools, test-taking experiences, and communities and community-building. The reflections and vignettes written by the authors and by Maggie, Elizabeth, Sophia, Nick, and the other teachers who contributed to this book are pieces of longer teaching autobiographies.

An educational philosophy represents your views on education and schooling, adolescents, learning, knowledge, and evaluation. It also describes your role in the classroom and definition and purpose of your subject area. An educational philosophy should also address many of the topics included in this book: teaching in a pluralistic society, definitions of curriculum, educational tools for middle and high school instruction, assessment and evaluation, and building community in culturally diverse settings.

A working portfolio usually includes documents that represent you, such as an educational autobiography and philosophy of teaching, and that highlight your accomplishments as you progress through your teacher education program. Moreover, it should include some of your attempts to address important issues related to instructional planning, implementation, and assessment. Some of the components of your portfolio might include your reflections on your strengths and weaknesses in the area of diversity, an outline of your experiences examining curriculum documents, an evaluation of curriculum resources, evidence of your proficiency with educational technology, your analysis of different methods of assessing your subject area, and plans for involving the community in your classroom.

## SUMMARY

This chapter focused on methods and strategies to help you experience success in the classroom throughout your professional career. The process of

professional growth begins with introspection as a means of better understanding yourself in and out of the classroom, and this chapter has outlined
a number of routes you might take to become the teacher you want to be.
Among the important points to remember are:

- The apprenticeship of observation is powerful but can be
  overcome through reflection on your own educational
  experiences and beliefs;
- Action research empowers teachers to construct knowledge about
  teaching and to revise practice;
- Professional colleagues, such as mentors and other novice teachers,
  are available to support your development as a teacher;
- Participation in higher education and in professional associations
  contributes to lifelong learning;
- The National Board for Professional Teaching Standards provides
  challenge and recognition for teachers who seek this certification.

## CONCLUSION

Inspirational quotes about teaching abound, but we authors especially like
this bit of counsel from Parker Palmer (1998):

> Teachers possess the power to create conditions that can help students learn a
> great deal–or keep them from learning much at all. Teaching is the intentional
> act of creating those conditions, and good teaching requires that we under-
> stand the inner sources of both the intent and the act. (p. 6)

Throughout this book, we have attempted to help you explore the inner
sources of teaching by sharing our own reflective, educational autobiographies and those of teachers we know. At the same time, teachers are public
servants and are accountable to their communities. A primary goal of this
book has been to demonstrate how effective professional practice is both
reflective and standards-based. We have used the standards for beginning
teaching developed by the Council of Chief State School Officers throughout
this book in order to make clear the connection between the inner and outer
landscapes of teaching. Reflection gives meaning to standards, and standards
give substance to reflection. We hope this book has set you on the path of
developing a reflective, standards-based practice.

# How to Use This Book with the CCSSO Model Standards for Beginning Teaching

| CCSSO Principle | Chapter Focus | Highlighted in Chapter |
|---|---|---|
| 1. The teacher understands the central concepts, tools of inquiry, and structures of the discipline(s) he or she teaches; and can create learning experiences that make these aspects of subject matter meaningful for students. | | 1, 5, 6, 7, 8, 9 |
| 2. The teacher understands how children learn and develop, and can provide learning opportunities that support their intellectual, social and personal development. | | 2, 8, 9, 11 |
| 3. The teacher understands how students differ in their approaches to learning and creates instructional opportunities that are adapted to diverse learners. | 2 | 1, 3, 5, 6, 8, 9, 10 |
| 4. The teacher understands and uses a variety of instructional strategies to encourage students' development of critical thinking, problem solving, and performance skills. | 6, 8, 9 | |
| 5. The teacher uses an understanding of individual and group motivation and behavior to create a learning environment that encourages positive social interaction, active engagement in learning, and self-motivation. | 3 | 1, 2, 7, 8, 9 |

| | CCSSO Principle | Chapter Focus | Highlighted in Chapter |
|---|---|---|---|
| 6. | The teacher uses knowledge of effective verbal, nonverbal, and media communication techniques to foster active inquiry, collaboration, and supportive interaction in the classroom. | | 3, 6, 7, 8, 9, 11 |
| 7. | The teacher plans instruction based upon knowledge of subject matter, students, community, and curriculum goals. | 4, 5 | 3, 6, 10, 11 |
| 8. | The teacher understands and uses formal and informal assessment strategies to evaluate and ensure the continuous intellectual, social, and physical development of the learners. | 10 | 4 |
| 9. | The teacher is a reflective practitioner who continually evaluates the effects of his/her choices and actions on others (students, parents, and other professionals in the learning community) and who actively seeks out opportunities to grow professionally. | 1, 12 | 7, 11 |
| 10. | The teacher fosters relationships with school colleagues, parents, and agencies in the larger community to support students' learning and well-being. | 11 | 4, 6, 12 |

# References

Adler, M. (1982). A revolution in education. *American Educator, 6*(4), 20–24.

Allen, D. (Ed.). (1998). *Assessing student learning: From grading to understanding.* New York: Teachers College Press.

Allen, M. G., & Stevens, R. L. (1997). *Middle grades social studies: Teaching and learning for active and responsible citizenship* (2nd ed.). Boston: Allyn & Bacon.

Apple, M. (1993). *Official knowledge.* New York: Routledge.

Applebee, A. N., Langer, J. A., Nystrand, M., & Gamoran, A. (2003). Discussion-based approaches to developing understanding: Classroom instruction and student performance in middle and high school English. *American Educational Research Journal, 40*(3), 685–730.

Armstrong, D. (2002). *Curriculum today.* Upper Saddle River, NJ: Prentice Hall.

Armstrong, T. (1994). *Multiple intelligences in the classroom.* Alexandria, VA: Association for Supervision and Curriculum Development.

Aronson, E., & Patnoe, S. (1997). *The jigsaw classroom: Building cooperation in the classroom* (2nd ed.). London: Longman.

Ausubel, D. P. (2000). *The acquisition and retention of knowledge: A cognitive view.* Boston: Kluwer.

Banks, J. A. (1994). *Multiethnic education: Theory and practice* (3rd ed.). Boston: Allyn & Bacon.

Banks, J., Cochran-Smith, M., Moll, L., Richert, A., Zeichner, K., LePage, P., Darling-Hammond, L., & Duffy, H. (2005). Teaching diverse learners. In L. Darling-Hammond & J. Bransford (Eds.), *Preparing teachers for a changing world: What teachers should learn and be able to do* (pp. 232–274). San Francisco: Jossey-Bass.

Bean, T. W., Readence, J. E., & Baldwin, R. S. (2008). *Content area literacy: An integrated approach* (9th ed.). Dubuque, IA: Kendall/Hunt.

Bennett, C. I. (2006). *Comprehensive multicultural education: Theory and practice* (6th ed.). Boston: Allyn & Bacon.

Berry, B., Hoke, M., & Hirsch, E. (2004). The search for highly qualified teachers. *Phi Delta Kappan, 85*(9), 684–689.

Berson, I., & Berson, M. J. (2009). Making sense of social studies with visualization tools. *Social Education, 73*(3), 124–126.

Bloom, B. S. (Ed.). (1956). *Taxonomy of educational objectives: The classification of education goals. Handbook I: Cognitive domain.* New York: Longmans, Green & Co.

Bloom, B. S., Madaus, G. F., & Hastings, J. T. (1981). *Evaluation to improve learning.* New York: McGraw-Hill.

Blumenfield, P. C., Marx, R. W., Soloway, E., & Krajik, J. (1996). Learning with peers: From small group cooperation to collaborative communities. *Educational Researcher, 25*(8), 37–40.

Boomer, G., Lester, N., Onore, C., & Cook, J. (Eds.). (1992). *Negotiating the curriculum: Educating for the 21st century.* Philadelphia: The Falmer Press.

Brandt, R. S. (1993). On teaching for understanding: A conversation with Howard Gardner. *Educational Leadership, 50*(7), 4–7.

Brandt, R. (1998). Listen first. *Educational Leadership, 55*(8), 25–30.

Brantlinger, E. A. (1993). *The politics of social class in secondary school: Views of affluent and impoverished youth.* New York: Teachers College Press.

Braun, J. A. (1999). Civic-moral development. In J. A. Braun & C. F. Risinger (Eds.), *Surfing social studies: The internet book* (pp. 137–147). Washington, DC: National Council for the Social Studies.

Brimijoin, K., Marquissee, E., & Tomlinson, C. A. (2003). Using data to differentiate instruction. *Educational Leadership, 60*(5), 70–73.

Bullough, R. V., Knowles, J. G., & Crow, N. A. (1991). *Emerging as a teacher.* New York: Routledge.

Burke, J. (2002). *Tools for thought: Graphic organizers for your classroom.* Portsmouth, NH: Heinemann.

Burstein, N., Sears, S., Wilcoxen, A., Cabello, B., & Spagna, M. (2004). Moving toward inclusive practices. *Remedial and Special Education, 25*(2), 104–116.

Callister, T. A., & Burbules, N. C. (2004). Just give it to me straight: A case against filtering the Internet. *Phi Delta Kappan, 85*(9), 649–655.

Camp, R. (1992). Portfolio reflections in middle and secondary classrooms. In K. B. Yancey (Ed.), *Portfolios in the writing classroom* (pp. 61–79). Urbana, IL: National Council of Teachers of English.

Canter, L., & Canter, M. (1992). *Assertive discipline.* Santa Monica, CA: Canter and Associates.

Carnegie Council on Adolescent Development. (1989). *Turning points: Preparing American youth for the 21st century.* New York: Carnegie Corporation.

Carter, C. J. (1997). Why reciprocal teaching? *Educational Leadership, 54*(6), 64–68.

Caskey, M. M., & Anfara, V. A., Jr. (2007). *Research summary: Young adolescents' developmental characteristics.* Retrieved July 15, 2009, from http://www.nmsa.org/Research/ResearchSummaries/DevelopmentalCharacteristics/tabod/1414/Default.aspx

Cavanagh, S. (2005). "Intelligent Design" goes on trial in Pa. *Education Week, 25*(6), 1, 16–17.

Charles, C. M., & Senter, G. W. (2004). *Building classroom discipline* (8th ed.). Boston: Allyn & Bacon.

Christenbury, L., & Kelly, P. (1983). *Questioning: A path to critical thinking.* Urbana, IL: National Council of Teachers of English.

Christensen, L. M., Wilson, E. K., Anders, S. K., Dennis, M. B., Kirkland, L., Beacham, M., & Warren, E. P. (2001, September/October). Teachers' reflection on their practice of social studies. *The Social Studies, 92*(5), 205–208.

Chuska, K. R. (1995). *Improving classroom questions: A teacher's guide to increasing students' motivation, participation, and higher-level thinking.* Bloomington, IN: Phi Delta Kappa Educational Foundation.

Cochran-Smith, M., & Lytle, S. L. (1993). *Inside outside: Teacher research and knowledge.* New York: Teachers College Press.

Cochran-Smith, M., & Lytle, S. L. (1996). Communities for teacher research: Fringe or forefront? In M. W. McLaughlin & I. Oberman (Eds.), *Teacher learning: New policies and practices* (pp. 92–114). New York: Teachers College Press.

Cohen, E. G., Kepner, D., & Swanson, P. (1995). Dismantling status hierarchies in heterogeneous classrooms. In J. Oakes & K. H. Quartz (Eds.), *Creating new educational communities, Ninety-fourth Yearbook of the National Society for the Study of Education, Part I* (pp. 16–31). Chicago: National Society for the Study of Education.

Coles, R. (1989). *The call of stories: Teaching and the moral imagination.* Boston: Houghton Mifflin.

Collier, J. L. (2005). *My brother Sam is dead.* New York: Scholastic Books.

Collier, J. L., & Collier, C. (1996). *With every drop of blood.* New York: Laurel-Leaf Press.

Commission on the Reorganization of Secondary Education. (1918). *Cardinal principles of secondary education.* Washington, DC: U.S. Government Printing Office.

Connelly, F. M., & Clandinin, D. J. (1990). Stories of experience and narrative inquiry. *Educational Researcher, 19*(5), 2–14.

Costa, A. L. (1990). Teacher behaviors that promote discussion. In W. W. Wilen (Ed.), *Teaching and learning through discussion* (pp. 45–78). Springfield, IL: Charles C. Thomas.

Council of Chief State School Officers. (1996). *Model standards for beginning teacher licensing, assessment and development: A resource for state dialogue.* Washington, DC: Author.

Crawford, S. B., Hicks, D., & Doherty, N. (2009). Worth the WAIT: Engaging social studies students with digital art. *Social Education, 73*(3), 136–139.

Cuban, L. (1996). Curriculum stability and change. In P. W. Jackson (Ed.), *Handbook of research on curriculum* (pp. 216–247). New York: Macmillan.

Cuban, L. (2003). *Oversold and underused.* Cambridge, MA: Harvard University Press.

Culatta, R. A., & Tompkins, J. R. (1999). *Fundamentals of special education: What every teacher needs to know.* Upper Saddle River, NJ: Merrill/Prentice Hall.

Davern, L. (1996). Listening to parents of children with disabilities. *Educational Leadership, 53*(7), 61–63.

Davidson, G. V. (1990). Matching learning styles with teaching styles: Is it a useful concept in instruction? *Performance and Instruction, 29*(4), 36–38.

Delpit, L. (1995). *Other people's children: Cultural conflict in the classroom.* New York: The New Press.

Dewey, J. (1933). *How we think: A restatement of the relation of reflective thinking to the educative process.* New York: D.C. Heath and Company.

Dicksinson, D. (1996). *Learning through many kinas of intelligence.* Retrieved August 8, 2006, from http://www.newhorizons.org/strategies/mi/dickinson_mi.html

Dryfoos, J. G. (1996). Full service schools. *Educational Leadership, 53*(7), 18–23.

Duhaney, L. M. G., & Duhaney, D. C. (2000). Assistive technology: Meeting the needs of learners with disabilities. *International Journal of Instructional Media, 27*(4), 393–401.

Echevarria, J., & Goldenberg, C. (1999). *Teaching secondary language minority students* [Research Brief #4]. Center for Research on Education, Diversity & Excellence, University of California, Santa Cruz.

Eckert, P. (1989). *Jocks and burnouts: Social categories and identity in the high school.* New York: Teachers College Press.

Educational Testing Service. (2004). *Study guide for principles of teaching and learning* (2nd ed.). Princeton, NJ: Author.

Edwards, C. H. (2003). *Classroom discipline and management* (4th ed.). San Francisco: Jossey-Bass.

Farr, B. P., & Trumbull, E. (1997). *Assessment alternatives for diverse classrooms.* Norwood, MA: Christopher-Gordon Publishers.

Fine, M., Burns, A., Payne, Y. A., & Torre, M. E. (2004). Civics lessons: The color and class of betrayal. *Teachers College Record, 106*(11), 2193–2223.

Finn, J. D. (1998). Parental engagement that makes a difference. *Educational Leadership, 55*(8), 20–24.

Fossey, R. (2008, August 18). "I support my gay friends": Free speech is alive and well in the school of the Florida Panhandle. *Teachers College Record.* Retrieved September 19, 2008, from http://www.tcrecord.org, ID Number 15349.

Friedland, E. S., & Truesdell, K. S. (2006). "I can read to whoever wants to hear me read": Buddy readers speak out with confidence. *Teaching Exceptional Children, 38*(5), 36–42.

Garcia, S. B., & Guerra, P. L. (2004). Deconstructing deficit thinking: Working with educators to construct more equitable learning environments. *Education and Urban Society, 36*(2), 150–168.

Gardner, H. (1993). *Multiple intelligences: The theory in practice.* New York: Basic Books.

Gardner, H. (1999). *Intelligence reframed: Multiple intelligences for the 21st century.* New York: Basic Books.

Gardner, J. (1995). Building a responsive community. In A. Etzioni (Ed.), *Rights and the common good. The communitarian perspective* (pp. 167–178). New York: St. Martin's Press.

Gay, G. (2000). *Culturally responsive teaching: Theory, research, and practice.* New York: Teachers College Press.

Gay, G. (2002). Preparing for culturally responsive teaching. *Journal of Teacher Education, 53*(2), 106–116.

Gay, G., & Kirkland, K. (2003). Developing critical consciousness and self-reflection in preservice teacher education. *Theory into Practice, 42*(3), 181–187.

Gere, A. R. (1985). *Roots in the sawdust: Writing to learn across the disciplines.* Urbana, IL: National Council of Teachers of English.

Gerver, R., Carter, C., Molina, D., Sgroi, R., Hansen, M., & Westergaard, S. (1998). *Algebra 2: An integrated approach.* Cincinnati, OH: Thomson South-Western.

Gest, T. (2000, October 9). Fixing your school: How five troubled high schools made dramatic turnarounds. *U.S. News & World Report,* pp. 65–73.

Giannett, C. C., & Sagarese, M. M. (1998). Turning parents from critics to allies. *Educational Leadership, 55*(8), 40–42.

Gladwell, M. (1999, August 2). The physical genius. *The New Yorker,* pp. 56–65.

Goldberger, S., & Kazis, R. (1996). Revitalizing high schools: What the school-to-career movement can contribute. *Phi Delta Kappan, 77*(8), 547–554.

Good, T. L., & Brophy, J. E. (2002). *Looking in classrooms* (9th ed.). Boston: Allyn & Bacon.

Goodrich, H. (1996/1997). Understanding rubrics. *Educational Leadership, 54*(4), 14–17.

Gordon, T. (1974). *Teacher effectiveness training.* New York: Peter H. Wyden.

Greene, M. (1993). The passions of pluralism: Multiculturalism and the expanding community. *Educational Researcher, 22*(1), 13–18.

Greenwood, S. C., & McCabe, P. P. (2008). How learning contracts motivate students. *Middle School Journal, 39*(5), 13–22.

Grossman, P. (1990). *The making of a teacher: Teacher knowledge and teacher education.* New York: Teachers College Press.

Grossman, P., Schonfeld, A., & Lee, C. (2005). Teaching subject matter. In L. Darling-Hammond & J. Bransford (Eds.), *Preparing teachers for a changing world: What teachers should learn and be able to do* (pp. 201–231). San Francisco: Jossey-Bass.

Grossman, P., Wineburg, S., & Woolworth, S. (2001). Toward a theory of teacher community. *Teachers College Record, 103*(6), 942–1012.

Guskey, T. R. (1996). Reporting on student learning: Lessons from the past–Prescriptions for the future. In T. R. Guskey (Ed.), *Communicating student learning* (pp. 13–24). Alexandria, VA: Association for Supervision and Curriculum Development.

Hackmann, D. G., Petzko, V. N., Valentine, J. W., Clark, D. C., Nori, J. R., & Lucas, S. E. (2002). Beyond interdisciplinary teaming: Findings and implications of the NASSP national middle level study. *NASSP Bulletin, 86*(632), 33–47.

Hadjioannou, X. (2007). Bringing the background to the foreground: What do classroom environments that support authentic discussions look like? *American Educational Research Journal, 44*(2), 370–399.

Hanson, F. A. (1993) *Testing, testing: Social consequences of the examined life.* Berkeley, CA: University of California Press.

Harmin, M., & Toth, M. (2006). *Inspiring active learning: A complete handbook.* Alexandria, VA: Association for Supervision and Curriculum Development.

Harris, D., & Yocum, M. (2000). *PASS: Powerful and authentic social studies education.* Silver Spring, MD: National Council for the Social Studies.

Harris, K. M., Gordon-Larsen, P., Chantala, K., & Udry, J. R. (2006). Longitudinal trends in race/ethnicity disparities in leading health indicators from adolescence to young adulthood. *Archives of Pediatrics and Adolescent Medicine, 160*(1), 74–81.

Heath, S. B. (1983). *Ways with words: Language, life and work in communities and classrooms.* New York: Cambridge University Press.

Heathcote, D., & Bolton, G. (1994). *Drama for learning: Dorothy Heathcote's mantle of the expert approach to education.* Portsmouth, NH: Heinemann.

Herman, J. L., Gearhart, M., & Aschbacher, P. R. (1996). Portfolios for classroom assessment: Design and implementation issues. In R. C. Calfee & P. Perfumo (Eds.), *Writing portfolios in the classroom: Policy and practice, promise and peril* (pp. 27–62). Mahwah, NJ: Lawrence Erlbaum.

Hill, B. C., & Ruptic, C. A. (1994). *Practical aspects of authentic assessment: Putting the pieces together.* Norwood, MA: Christopher-Gordon Publishers.

Hilliard, A. G. III. (1990). Misunderstanding and testing intelligence. In J. I. Goodlad & P. Keating (Eds.), *Access to knowledge* (pp. 145–158). New York: College Board.

Hodgkinson, H. (2003). *Leaving too many children behind: A demographer's view on the neglect of America's youngest children.* Washington, DC: Institute for Educational Leadership.

Hollingshead, D. A. (1995). *Postethnic America: Beyond multiculturalism.* New York: Basic Books.

International Society for Technology in Education. (2008). *National educational technology standards for teachers.* Eugene, OR: Author.

Jacob, B. A. (2002). *Accountability, incentives and behavior: The impact of high-stakes testing in the Chicago Public Schools.* National Bureau of Economic Research, Working Paper No. 8968.

Jacobson, L. (2004). First major study suggests worth of national "seal." *Education Week, 23*(47), 1–3.

Jarolimek, J. (1991, January/February). Focus on concepts: Teaching for meaningful learning. *Social Studies and the Young Learner,* pp. 3–5.

Jersild, A. T. (1955). *When teachers face themselves.* New York: Teachers College, Columbia University.

Joseph, P. B., & Efron, S. (2005, March). Seven worlds of moral education. *Phi Delta Kappan, 86*(7), 525–533

Joyce, B. R., Weil, M., & Calhoun, E. (2004). *Models of teaching* (7th ed.). Boston: Allyn & Bacon.

Kahne, J., & Westheimer, J. (1996). In the service of what? The politics of service learning. *Phi Delta Kappan, 77*(9), 592–599.

Kellough, R., & Carjuzza, J. (2008). *Teaching in the middle and secondary schools* (9th ed.). Upper Saddle River, NJ: Prentice Hall.

Kentucky Department of Education. (1998). *How to develop a standards-based unit of study.* Frankfort, KY: Author.

Kimbrell-Lee, J., & Wood, T. (1994). The inclusive writing workshop. In M. Dalheim (Ed.), *Toward inclusive classrooms* (pp. 39–52). Washington, DC: National Education Association.

Kinchin, I. M. (2000). Concept mapping in biology. *Journal of Biological Education, 34*(2), 61–68.

King, S. H., & Goodwin, A. L. (2002). *Culturally responsive parental involvement: Concrete understandings and basic strategies.* New York: American Association of Colleges for Teacher Education.

King-Sears, M. E., & Cummings, C. S. (1996). Inclusive practices of classroom teachers. *Remedial and Special Education, 17*(4), 217–225.

Klass, D. (1996). *California blue.* New York: Scholastic.

Klein, S. (2007). *Handbook for achieving gender equity through education* (2nd ed.). New York: Routledge.

Kohn, A. (2006). *Beyond discipline: From compliance to community* (10th ed.). Alexandria, VA: Association for Supervision and Curriculum Development.

Kottler, J. A., Zehm, S. J., & Kottler, E. I. (2005). *On being a teacher: The human dimension* (3rd ed.). Thousand Oaks, CA: Corwin.

Kounin, J. S. (1977). *Discipline and group management in classrooms.* Malabar, FL: R. E. Krieger.

Kozioff, M. A., La Nunziata, L., Cowardin, L., & Bessellieu, F. B. (2001). Direct instruction: Its contributions to high school achievement. *The High School Journal, 84*(2), 54–71.

Kozol, J. (1991). S*avage inequalities: Children in America's schools.* New York: Crown.

Kozol, J. (2001). *Ordinary resurrections: Children in the years of hope.* New York: Harper Perennial.

Kuriloff, P. (2000, April 28). If John Dewey were alive today, he'd be a webhead. *Chronicle of Higher Education, 46*(34), A72.

Ladson-Billings, G. (1994). *The dreamkeepers: Successful teachers of African American children.* San Francisco: Jossey-Bass.

Ladson-Billings, G. (2001). *Crossing over to Canaan: The journey of new teachers in diverse classrooms.* San Francisco: Jossey-Bass.

Lakoff, G., & Johnson, M. (1980). *Metaphors we live by.* Chicago: University of Chicago Press.

Lawrence-Brown, D. (2004). Differentiated instruction: Inclusive strategies for standards-based learning that benefit the whole class. *American Secondary Education, 32*(3), 34–62.

Lewis, A. C. (2005). States feel the crunch of NCLB. *Phi Delta Kappan, 70*(5), 70–71.

Lieberman, A., & McLaughlin, M. W. (1996). Networks for educational change: Powerful and problematic. In M. W. McLaughlin & I. Oberman (Eds.), *Teacher learning: New policies, new practices* (pp. 63–72). New York: Teachers College Press.

Little, J. W. (2003). Inside teacher community: Representations of classroom practice. *Teachers College Record, 105*(6), 913–945.

Lortie, D. C. (1975). *Schoolteacher: A sociological study.* Chicago: University of Chicago Press.

Mackenzie, J. (2000). *Beyond technology: Questioning, research, and the information literate school.* Bellingham, WA: FNO Press.

Madaus, G. F., & Kellaghan, T. (1996). Curriculum evaluation and assessment. In P. W. Jackson (Ed.), *Handbook of research on curriculum* (pp. 119–156). New York: Macmillan.

Mager, R. F. (1997). *Preparing instructional objectives* (3rd ed.). Atlanta, GA: Center for Effective Performance.

Mandel, S. M. (2003). *Cooperative work groups: Preparing students for the real world.* Thousand Oaks, CA: Corwin.

Marzano, R. J. (2006). *Classroom assessment and grading that work.* Alexandria, VA: Association for Supervision and Curriculum Development.

Marzano, R. J., Pickering, D. J., & Pollack, J. E. (2001). *Classroom instruction that works: Research-based strategies for increasing student achievement.* Alexandria, VA: Association for Supervision and Curriculum Development.

McCullough, K. (1999). New teachers enthusiastic about TEACH2000. *The Council Chronicle, 9*(2), 1, 7.

McLaughlin, H. J. (1994). From negation to negotiation: Moving away from the management metaphor. *Action in Teacher Education, 16*(4), 75–84.

McLaughlin, M. W., & Talbert, J. E. (1993). *Contexts that matter for teaching and learning: Strategic opportunities for meeting the nation's educational goals.* Palo Alto, CA: Center for Research on the Contexts of Secondary School Teaching.

Meier, D. (2002). *The power of their ideas: Lessons for America from a small school in Harlem.* New York: Beacon.

Meister, D., & Melnick, S. (2004). National new teacher study: Beginning teachers' concerns. *Action in Teacher Education, 24*(4), 87–94.

Mertler, C. A. (2004). *Using standardized tests data to guide instruction and intervention.* Retrieved June 20, 2006, from http://www.ericdigests.org/2003-4/standardized-test.html

Michaels, S., O'Connor, C., & Resnick, L. B. (2008). Deliberative discourse idealized and realized: Accountable talk in the classroom and in civic life. *Studies in the Philosophy of Education, 27*(1), 283–297.

Milone, M., & Saltpepper, J. (1996). Technology and equity issues. *Technology and Learning, 16*(4), 38–42.

Moffett, J. (1988). *Storm in the mountains: A case study of censorship, conflict, and consciousness.* Carbondale, IL: Southern Illinois University Press.

Moore, D. W., Bean, T. W., Birdyshaw, D., & Rycik, J. A. (1999). *Adolescent literacy: A position statement.* Newark, DE: International Reading Association.

Murray, D. M. (2001). *Write to learn* (7th ed.). Belmont, CA: Heinle Publishing.

National Center for Fair and Open Testing. (2006). *Fact sheets.* Retrieved July 20, 2006, from http://www.fairtest.org

National Commission on Teaching and America's Future. (2003). *No dream denied: A pledge to America's children.* Washington, DC: Author.

National Commission on Writing in America's Schools and Colleges. (2003). *The neglected "R": The need for a writing revolution.* New York: College Entrance Examination Board.

National Council for Teachers of Mathematics. (1989). *Curriculum and evaluation standards for school mathematics.* Reston, VA: Author.

National Council for the Social Studies. (1994). *Curriculum standards for social studies: Expectations for excellence.* Washington, DC: Author.

National Council for the Social Studies Task Force on Ethnic Studies Curriculum Guidelines. (1991). *Curriculum guidelines for multicultural education.* Washington, DC: Author.

National Council of Teachers of English. (1996). *Guidelines for selection of material in English language arts programs.* Urbana, IL: Author.

National Education Association of the United States, Commission on the Reorganization of Secondary Education. (1918). *Cardinal principles of secondary education.* Washington, DC: U.S. Government Printing Office.

Negroponte, N. (1995). *Being digital.* New York: Knopf.

Newmann, F. M., Marks, H. M., & Gamoran, A. (1996). Authentic pedagogy and student performance. *American Journal of Education, 104*(4), 280–312.

Nieto, S. (2003). *Affirming diversity: The sociopolitical context of multicultural education* (4th ed.). Boston, MA: Allyn & Bacon.

Noddings, N. (1997). Thinking about standards. *Phi Delta Kappan, 79*(3), 184–189.

Nolen, A. L., & Vander Putten, J. (2007). Action research in education: Addressing gaps in ethical principles and practices. *Educational Researcher, 36*(7), 401–407.

Oakes, J. (1985). *Keeping track: How schools structure inequality.* New Haven, CT: Yale University Press.

Osguthorpe, R. D. (2008). On the reasons we want teachers of good disposition and moral character. *Journal of Teacher Education, 9*(4), 288–299.

Ostling, R. N. (2001, May 19). *Researcher tabulates world's believers.* Retrieved July 15, 2009, from http://www.sltrib.com/May/05192001/Saturday/98497.htm

Palmer, P. J. (1998). *The courage to teach: Exploring the inner landscape of a teacher's life.* San Francisco: Jossey-Bass.

Paris, S. G., & Ayres, L. R. (1994). *Becoming reflective students and teachers with portfolios and authentic assessment.* Washington, DC: American Psychological Association.

Parker, W. (1988). Thinking to learn concepts. *Social Studies, 79*(2), 70–73.

Paterson, P. O., & Elliott, L. N. (2006). Struggling reader to struggling reader: High school students' responses to a cross-age tutoring program. *Journal of Adolescent and Adult Literacy, 49*(5), 378–389.

Paul, J. R., & Kaiser, C. (1996). Do women live longer than men? Investigating grave-yard data with computers. *Learning and Leading with Technology, 23*(8), 13–15.

Paulson, F. L., & Paulson, P. R. (1992). The varieties of self-reflection. *Portfolio News, 4*(1), 1, 10–14.

Paulson, F. L., Paulson, P. R., & Meyer, C. A. (1991). What makes a portfolio a port-folio? *Educational Leadership, 51*(5), 38–42.

Perkins, D. N. (1995). *Smart schools: From training memories to educating minds.* New York: The Free Press.

Peshkin, A. (1991). *The color of strangers, the color of friends: The play of ethnicity in school and community.* Chicago: University of Chicago Press.

Petto, S. G. (1998). Art and service learning: Connection within a community of shared experience. *Network, 7*(2), 1–3.

Polite, V. C., & Adams, A. H. (1997). Critical thinking and values clarification through Socratic seminars. *Urban Education, 32*(2), 256–278.

Powell, A. G., Farrar, E., & Cohen, D. (1986). *The shopping mall high school: Winners and losers in the educational marketplace.* Boston: Houghton Mifflin.

Powell, R. R., Zehm, S., & Garcia, J. (1996). *Field experience: Strategies for exploring diversity in schools.* Upper Saddle River, NJ: Merrill/Prentice-Hall.

Pruitt, D. (2000). *Your adolescent: Emotional, behavioral, and cognitive development from early adolescence through the teen years.* New York: HarperCollins.

Putnam, R. D. (2000). *Bowling alone: The collapse and revival of American community.* New York: Simon & Schuster.

Ravitch, D., & Finn, C. E. Jr. (1989). *What do our 17-year-olds know? A report on the first national assessment of history and literature.* New York: Harper & Row.

Reigeluth, C. M. (1997). Educational standards: To standardize or to customize learn-ing? *Phi Delta Kappan, 79*(3), 202–206.

Ressler, P., & Chase, B. (2009). Sexual identity and gender variance: Meeting the educational challenges. *English Journal, 90*(4), 15–22.

Rich, D. (1998). What parents want from teachers. *Educational Leadership, 55*(8), 37–39.

Rief, S. F. (1996). *How to reach and teach all children in the inclusive classroom.* San Fran-cisco: Jossey-Bass.

Rock, M. L. (2004). Graphic organizers: Tools to build behavioral literacy and foster emotional competency. *Intervention in School and Clinic, 40*(1), 10–37.

Rogers, D. L., & Babinski, L. (1999). Breaking through isolation with new teacher groups. *Educational Leadership, 56*(8), 38–40.

Rosenshine, B. (1995). Advances in research on instruction. *Journal of Educational Research, 88*(5), 262–268.

Rosenshine, B., & Meister, C. (1994). Reciprocal teaching: A review of the research. *Review of Educational Research, 64*(4), 479–530.

Rousseau, C., & Tate, W. E. (2003). No time like the present: Reflecting on equity in school mathematics. *Theory into Practice, 42*(3), 210–216.

Rowe, M. B. (1986). Wait time: Slowing down may be a way of speeding up! *Journal of Teacher Education, 37*(1), 43–50.

Sadker, D. M. (2000). Gender equity: Still knocking at the classroom door. *Equity and Excellence in Education, 33*(1), 80–83.

Sapon-Shevin, M. (1995). *Playing favorites: Gifted education and the disruption of classroom community.* Albany: State University of New York Press.

Sarason, S. B. (1993). *You are thinking of teaching? Opportunities, problems, realities.* San Francisco: Jossey-Bass.

Savage, T. V., Savage, M. K., & Armstrong, D. G. (2005). *Teaching in the secondary school: An introduction* (6th ed.). Upper Saddle River, NJ: Merrill/Prentice Hall.

Savoie, J. M., & Hughes, A. S. (1994). Problem-based learning as classroom solution. *Educational Leadership, 52*(3), 54–57.

Saye, J. W. (1998). Creating time to develop student thinking: Team-teaching with technology. *Social Education, 62*(6), 356–362.

Scala, M. C. (2001). *Working together: Reading and writing in inclusive classrooms.* Newark, DE: International Reading Association.

Scales, P. C., Foster, K. C., Mannes, M., Horst, M. A., Pinto, K. C., & Rutherford, A. (2005). School-business partnerships, developmental assets, and positive outcomes among urban high school students: A mixed-methods study. *Urban Education, 40*(2), 144–189

Schön, D. A. (1987). *Educating the reflective practitioner.* San Francisco: Jossey-Bass.

Shields, C. J. (1993). Learning styles: Where Jung, the Beatles, and schools intersect. *Curriculum Review, 33*(2), 9–12.

Shriner, J. G., Ysseldyke, J. E., Thurlow, M. L., & Honetschlager, D. (1994). "All" means "All"–Including students with disabilities. *Educational Leadership, 51*(6), 38–42.

Shulman, L. (1987). Knowledge and teaching: Foundations of the new reform. *Harvard Educational Review, 57*(1), 1–22.

Silberman, M. L. (1996). *Active learning: 101 strategies to teach any subject.* Boston: Allyn & Bacon.

Silver, H. F., Strong, R. W., & Perini, M. J. (2000). *So each may learn: Integrating learning styles and multiple intelligences.* Alexandria, VA: Association for Supervision and Curriculum Development.

Siskin, L. S., & Little, J. W. (Eds.). (1995). *The subjects in question: Departmental organization and the high school.* New York: Teachers College Press.

Sizer, T. (2003, April 23). Two reports. *Education Week, 22*(32), 24, 25, 36.

Slavin, R. E. (1995). *Cooperative learning: Theory, research and practice* (2nd ed.). Boston: Allyn & Bacon.

Slavin, R. E., & Calderon, M. (2001). *Effective programs for Latino students.* Mahwah, NJ: Lawrence Erlbaum Associates.

Slavkin, M. L. (2004). *Authentic learning: How learning about the brain can shape the development of students.* Lanham, MD: Scarecrow Education.

Smagorinsky, P., Cook, L. S., & Johnson, T. S. (2003). The twisting path of concept development in learning to teach. *Teachers College Record, 105*(8), 1399–1436.

Smagorinsky, P., Cook, L. S., Moore, C., Jackson, A., & Fry, P. G. (2004). Tensions in learning to teach: Accommodation and the development of a teaching identity. *Journal of Teacher Education, 55*(1), 8–24.

Smith, R. E., & Manley, S. A. (1994). Social studies learning activities packets. *Social Studies, 85*(4), 160–164.

Spalding, E., & Wilson, A. (2002). Demystifying reflection: A study of pedagogical strategies that encourage reflective journal writing. *Teachers College Record, 104*(7), 1393–1421.

Stainback, S., Stainback, W., & Slavin, R. (1989). Classroom organization for diversity among students. In S. Stainback, W. Stainback, & M. Forest (Eds.), *Educating all students in the mainstream of regular education* (pp. 131–142). Baltimore, MD: Paul Brooks.

Stevenson, C. (2002). *Teaching ten to fourteen year olds* (3rd ed.). Boston: Allyn & Bacon.

Stiggins, R. J. (2004). *Student involved assessment FOR learning* (4th ed.). Upper Saddle River, NJ: Prentice Hall.

Story, C. (1998). What instructional designers need to know about advance organizers. *International Journal of Instructional Media, 25*(3), 253–261.

Strichart, S. S., Mangrum, C. T., & Iannuzzi, P. (2001). *Teaching study skills and strategies to students with learning disabilities, attention deficit disorders, or special needs* (3rd ed.). Boston: Allyn & Bacon.

Swift, J., Gooding, C., & Swift, P. (1988). Questions and wait time. In J. Dillon (Ed.), *Questioning and discussion: A multidisciplinary study* (pp. 192–212). Norwood, NJ: Ablex.

Tanner, D., & Tanner, L. (2006). *Curriculum development: Theory into practice* (4th ed.). Upper Saddle River, NJ: Merrill/Prentice Hall.

Tanner, M. L., & Casados, L. (1998). Promoting and studying discussions in math classes. *Journal of Adolescent and Adult Literacy, 41*(5), 1081–2004.

Tatum, B., & McWhorter, P. (1999). Maybe not everything, but a whole lot you always wanted to know about mentoring. In P. Graham, S. Hudson-Ross, C. Adkins, P. McWhorter, & J. McDuffie Stewart (Eds.), *Teacher/mentor: A dialogue for collaborative learning* (pp. 21–33). New York: Teachers College Press.

Tauber, R. (2007). *Classroom management: Sound theory and effective practice* (4th ed.). Westport, CT: Praeger.

Thorkildsen, R., & Scott Stein, M. R. (1998). *Is parent involvement related to student achievement? Exploring the evidence* [Research Bulletin No. 22, Center for Evaluation, Development, and Research]. Bloomington, IN: Phi Delta Kappa.

Tiedt, P. L., & Tiedt, I. M. (2001). *Multicultural teaching: A handbook of activities, information and resources* (6th ed.). Boston: Allyn & Bacon.

Tishman, S., Perkins, D., & Jay, E. (1994). *The thinking classroom: Learning and teaching in a culture of thinking.* Boston: Allyn & Bacon.

Tomlinson, C. A., & Doubet, K. (2005). Reach them to teach them. *Educational Leadership, 62*(7), 8–15.

Tomlinson, C. A. (2001). *How to differentiate instruction in mixed-ability classrooms* (2nd ed.). Alexandria, VA: Association for Supervision and Curriculum Development.

Townsend, A. (2001). A high school senior asks, "Who makes our graduation gowns?" *Rethinking Schools, 15*(30). Retrieved January 21, 2005, from http://www.rethinkingschools.org

Traver, R. (1998, March). What is a good guiding question? *Educational Leadership, 55,* 70–73.

Tredway, L. (1995, September). Socratic seminars: Engaging students in intellectual discourse. *Educational Leadership, 53,* 26–29.

Tyler, R. W. (1979). Specific approaches to curriculum development. In J. R. Gress & D. E. Purpel (Eds.), *Curriculum: An introduction to the field* (pp. 239–254). Berkeley, CA: McCutchan.

U.S. Department of Education. (2003). *Meeting the highly qualified teacher challenge: The Secretary's second annual report on teacher quality.* Washington, DC: Author.

U.S. Department of Education, National Center for Education Statistics. (2003). *Digest of education statistics, 2003.* Washington, DC: Author.

Vacca, R. T., Vacca, J. L., & Bruneau, B. (1997). Teachers reflecting on practice. In J. Flood, S. B. Heath, & D. Lapp (Eds.), *Handbook of research on teaching literacy through the communicative and visual arts* (pp. 445–450). New York: Macmillan.

Valli, L. (Ed.). (1990). *Reflective teacher education: Cases and critiques.* Albany: State University of New York Press.

Vermette, P. J. (1997). *Making cooperative learning work: Student teams in K–12 classrooms.* Upper Saddle River, NJ: Merrill/Prentice-Hall.

Viadero, D. (2004, April 7). High school course loads tougher, study says. *Education Week, 23*(30), 12.

Walberg, H. J., & Paik, S. J. (2004). Effective general practices. In G. Cawelti (Ed.), *Handbook of research on improving student achievement* (3rd ed., pp. 25–37). Arlington, VA: Educational Research Service.

Wang, J., & Odell, S. J. (2002). Mentored learning to teach according to standards-based reform: A critical review. *Review of Educational Research, 72*(3), 481–546.

Wenger, E. C., & Snyder, W. M. (2000). Communities of practice: The organizational frontier. *Harvard Business Review, 78*(1), 139–145.

Wiggins, G. P. (1993). *Assessing student performance: Exploring the purpose and limits of testing.* San Francisco: Jossey-Bass.

Wiggins, G. P., & McTighe, J. (2005). *Understanding by design* (2nd ed.). Alexandria, VA: Association for Supervision and Curriculum Development.

Wilen, W. W. (1991). *Questioning skills for teachers* (3rd ed.). Washington, DC: National Education Association.

Willard, N. (2003). Off-campus, harmful online student speech. *Journal of School Violence, 2*(1), 65–93.

Willems, A. L., McConnell, R., & Willems, E. M. (1997). Middle school students, teachers, and parents contracting for success. *Journal of Instructional Psychology, 24*(4), 246–252.

Williams, B. (2005). Taken on faith: Religion and identity in writing classes. *Journal of Adolescent and Adult Literacy, 48*(6), 514–518.

Willis, S. (1995). When parents object to classroom practice: Resolving conflicts over techniques, materials. *Education Update, 37*(1), 1, 6–8.

Wraga, W. G. (2002). Renewing the comprehensive high school. *Principal Leadership, 2*(8), 33–37.

Xie, Y., & Shauman, K. A. (2003). *Women in science: Career processes and outcomes.* Cambridge, MA: Harvard University Press.

Zeichner, K. M., & Liston, D. P. (1987). Teaching student teachers to reflect. *Harvard Educational Review, 57*(1), 23–48.

# Index

# About the Authors

**Elizabeth Spalding** is an associate professor in the Department of Curriculum and Instruction at the University of Nevada, Las Vegas, where she teaches courses in English education. She is an active member of the National Council of Teachers of English (NCTE), past president of the Kentucky Council of Teachers of English, and former director of a National Writing Project site. She was project manager for standards at the NCTE in Urbana, Illinois, where she worked on the development of the national standards for English language arts. Prior to earning her doctoral degree from Indiana University–Bloomington, she was a classroom teacher for 14 years.

**Jesus Garcia** is professor of Social Studies Education at the University of Nevada, Las Vegas and former president of the National Council for the Social Studies. He is co-author of *Social Studies for Children: A Guide to Basic Instruction* and *McDougal Littell's American History Program*. Dr. Garcia received his doctoral degree from the University of California, Berkeley. He taught elementary and secondary school in Fremont and in San Jose, California.

**Joseph A. Braun, Jr.** was an elementary educator for 7 years before earning a doctorate in Curriculum & Instruction from Northern Illinois University. He was a professor of social studies education for 29 years, holding faculty positions at the University of Wyoming, CSU–Chico, and Illinois State University. Retiring as a professor emeritus in 2003, he and his wife relocated to Carmel, California, where he continues to teach online courses for the University of Missouri and serve as the coordinator of Professional Development for the National Council for the Social Studies.